Gourmet ON A HOT PLATE

TINY KITCHEN TIPS & RECIPES

By
Judy Alter
Author of *Cooking My Way Through Life With Kids and Books* and other titles

Alter Ego Press
Fort Worth, Texas 76110
http://www.judyalter.com
j.alter@tcu.edu

Editor: Carol Roark
Design: Amy Balamut
With thanks to
Susan Wittig Albert for enthusiastic support of this project
Subie Green and Gayla Christiansen for title advice
Heather Hogan Holt for recipe advice
Many friends who ate my experiments and gave me mostly honest reactions

TABLE OF CONTENTS

WHY I'M COOKING ON A HOT PLATE

During our family Christmas holiday in 2015 my four children and I sat around an outdoor fire and discussed the future—my future. I was in full control of my senses and my life, happily living in my home of twenty-five years, pursuing my writing career, and enjoying retirement with friends and family. I dined in restaurants a lot, drove an aging but cute Volkswagen convertible, loved on my dog, and thought life was peachy—except for the worsening pain in my low back and left hip, which gave me an increasing fear of falling and lack of balance. But I was pushing eighty, and it was time to look ahead.

Jordan and Christian offered, and everyone else accepted, that they and grandson Jacob would move to my house. It made sense for a lot of reasons—Jacob's school is across the street, their work is closer, Jordan loves my old house. Christian loved their house—in a relatively new addition (a twenty-five-year-old house is relatively new to me), and I think he and Jacob left it reluctantly. But Christian said, "It's what you do for family." We considered and discarded the idea of converting the garage/guest house into a master bedroom suite, which would leave Jacob in the house with me. Ultimate decision: the existing structure would become my cottage. Work began in the late spring of 2016. And I moved into my new quarters in September.

Little did we know that happy Christmas what lay around the bend for me: a broken ankle that led to a series of health challenges. My kids were alarmed, though I didn't realize that until I emerged at the other end of my long journey. By January 2017, my ankle had healed but in an odd configuration. I had complicated revision surgery on my left hip, which had totally disintegrated, and I slowly began the long road to recovery. By then I was ensconced in my cottage. My cozy space is perfect for me—a combination office/living room where I can and do entertain guests, and an upscale bathroom with a wonderful shower. The bedroom barely holds my antique bed and one marble-topped buffet that I use as a chest of drawers, but it does have a large walk-in closet. There is also a postage-stamp but efficient kitchen.

The kitchen of course is the problem. Size dictated that it be small, so it is way short on counter space. A bigger complication: local zoning laws forbid more than one full kitchen on a property. That means I cannot have built-in appliances such as a stove or dishwasher. Anything you plug in is okay, so I have a large refrigerator, toaster oven, magnetic hot plate, and coffee maker.

Over several months, Jordan and I did a massive down-sizing of my belongings—clothes, books, kitchen things, you name it. Antiques and things with family significance were spread among the kids and my brother. To this day, the thing I miss most is my kitchen utensils, though there's that occasional sweater or top that I wonder about.

My four kids and their families came one weekend for the great move-in, shooed me into the house, and moved all my things in by six o'clock that night (movers came for slightly less than two hours to do the heavy furniture). Bookshelves were filled (I had given away or sold tons of books), pictures hung, clothes in the closet, and kitchen cupboards full.

I settled into the cottage as I made slow but steady progress recovering. For the first seven or eight months I barely cared what was in the kitchen. I made toast and cereal for breakfast, maybe tuna salad for lunch, and ate whatever Jordan fixed for supper. She did most of my cooking, dishwashing, everything, and her crown shines to this day. But gradually I began to reclaim my kitchen. At my four months post-op hip checkup, I told the doctor I was writing again, cooking again, and wearing make-up—all signs of healing.

Indeed, I published a novella, *The Color of Fear,* in May 2017. An addition to the Kelly O'Connell Mysteries, it served to prove to me and demonstrate to the world that I could still write. And I cooked—mostly elaborate appetizers—but I made spaghetti sauce from scratch, fettucine with smoked salmon for a lunch guest, a salmon loaf (sent it in to the house for baking), beans on toast, mushrooms on toast, Welsh rarebit, and other main dishes for guests. I regularly cooked squash, corn, green beans, and other veggies for myself. My repertoire kept growing, and I was having fun in the kitchen again.

The idea for this cookbook came about gradually as this friend and that suggested I write about my kitchen experiences. Believe me, there were some negatives. I regularly burned things, even in the toaster oven, which set off the smoke alarm more than once. The smoke alarm hurts my dog's ears, and she associates it with the toaster, so Sophie now begins barking when she sees me with a slice of bread in my hands. I drop things constantly, mostly because I still must chop and stir while seated.

What pushed me over the edge was friend Subie Green's suggestion of a title: *Gourmet on a Hot Plate.* I began with a sort of trial run—a cooking column in the neighborhood newsletter which, conveniently, I edit. This book grew from that column and from my continuing experiments in my tiny kitchen.

Some random thoughts on tiny kitchen cooking

Despite the title, this is not so much about cooking on a hot plate as it is the idea of cooking and entertaining in a small space without oven, stove, or microwave. Surely there are many other people, both young and old, who face the same challenges my tiny kitchen offered. Different folks will want different appliances—I can get along pretty well without a microwave. My oldest daughter suggested that since I never used it we should put the microwave in the closet (which was rapidly getting crowded). Thereafter she spent the week she was with us running into the house to microwave her lunch or dinner—she was her own best contradiction. I also get along without a full-size crockpot or food processor (however, you couldn't pry me away from my small one), but I'm lucky. I can borrow those from the house (just across the backyard) whenever I need. I can also on occasion send dishes into the main house to be baked, but I don't do that often.

The two criteria that determine what you need in your tiny kitchen are space and time. Working all day? You may well want that slow cooker or the InstaPot. Retired and setting your own schedule? You can take all day to cook a pot of soup if you want. A third factor, or some variant of it, may be the way you like to cook. I'm an old-fashioned cook who enjoys being in the kitchen, I want to know my ingredients, follow the process. You may really hate to cook and welcome every new convenience that comes along. Not a bad thing at all.

My hot plate is at the center of my cooking. I have learned to do all kind of things on it. I've also learned that it cooks hot and fast—and you have to push the start button. That was a biggie. The first time I used it, I set the temperature I wanted and waited for the pan to heat. Jordan was with me. We put a lamb chop in the pan. Nothing. No sizzle. She'd hold her hand out to feel heat, put her ear down, poke the meat. Nothing. Then we saw the start button.

The hot plate, which operates magnetically, requires special pots and pans, which of course you buy from the company that sold you the hot plate.

Gone, with regret, are the days of cooking in a cast-iron skillet. These new pots and pans will scorch food if you turn your back, but they are super easy to clean, and I have one large pot in which I can simmer a pot of soup all day. There is one setting on the hot plate so low that you doubt it's cooking. Works great for simmering.

So I value my hot plate, but I don't need or want a lot of today's modern gadgets. That may be due to the limitations of space but also to my inclinations as one who's been cooking close to seventy years—yes, I started young. Cooking without gadgets lets you really get in touch with the ingredients of your food. So does making your own soup, casserole, whatever from scratch. I do not use "low fat" or "no fat" ingredients because as someone pointed out to me that label translates into a shit-storm of chemicals. I am still trying to convince one son that aspartame in diet drinks is doing him irreparable harm—even the threat of dementia doesn't seem to deter him. I try to avoid processed foods which are probably a greater temptation than ever in the tiny kitchen. For instance, you'll find a recipe here for taco seasoning, because who needs the salt, sugar, and preservatives found in the commercial products? I will admit to using some soup mixes and prepared products like crescent dinner rolls in a tube, particularly for appetizers.

Simplicity may be the key to cooking in a small space. It's certainly not about cooking an elaborate recipe, and I've learned to turn a blind eye to a lot of wonderful but complicated recipes in the many cooking magazines to which I subscribe. You won't find my $8,000 Leg of Lamb Recipe here. My daughter and a neighbor recently collaborated on it, using my recipe, and it was delicious. I couldn't have cooked it in the cottage.

I've left out most of the recipes that were in my first cookbook, *Cooking My Way Through Life with Kids and Books* (you can find the $8,000 Leg of Lamb there). Those were the days I was cooking for Coxey's Army, sometimes twenty at the table. I've also left out recently discovered recipes for big meals and things that are impractical in a toaster oven.

Most of these recipes serve two to four. I haven't always indicated the number of servings, because I don't know your appetite. My idea of one serving may be only a plate half full for you. The heartiest meal here is a marvelous cheesy beef-and-noodle casserole that I can't resist. I've included it because I suspect you can occasionally pack a crowd into your tiny space.

This cookbook is like a cafeteria line—take what you want. Choices will vary for each person. What you will find on these pages are recipes that reflect my changing tastes—I am somewhat of a cross between gourmet and down-home cook. There are lots of appetizers and light meals, because that's the way I like to eat. Tapas were created for me. I like strong flavors and fish—pickled herring, smoked salmon, lots of tuna. I don't like hot spices, so I temper a lot of Mexican dishes. Neither my taste buds nor my stomach can tolerate bell peppers. They appear in some recipes here, but are strictly optional.

Cooking small may be more work—what you'd do in one batch in a traditional kitchen, you may do in several small batches in a tiny kitchen. And you'll do more "loads" of dishes rather than let them pile up. Being in a rush is incompatible. Wish I'd learned that lesson forty years ago.

What you do need

Again, this is up to individual choice, but here are the choices I've made:

A good, roomy toaster oven with several functions

A magnetic hot plate and the pans to go with it

A coffee pot (I like my Keurig, now out of fashion, because I can do tea as well as coffee)

A counter-top food processor—mine does not sit on the counter top but resides in a deep drawer for space reasons

A hand-held mixer

A colander

A wooden salad bowl

Things I don't need but you might

An InstaPot—I actually have one, have used it once, but gave it to Jordan and Christian. I have no space for it, find the learning curve steep, and, because I'm retired, I can take all day to make a pot of soup if I wish.

An Air Fryer—probably I don't understand the benefits of these, but my first instinct is to state that I don't eat much fried food.

A blender—I don't know what I'd do with one that I cannot do with my small processor.

A slow cooker or crockpot—I have a small, single-serving crockpot and have never used it. A large pot is part of the cookware set that came with the hot plate, and I use it for everything from pasta to soup.

A grill—I had an indoor grill in the kitchen and used it frequently; I miss it in the cottage, but there's simply no space. I find an outdoor grill to be too much trouble, so I do without; if ever desperate, I can ask Christian to grill for me.

A microwave—I rarely if ever cooked in a microwave but only used it to reheat leftovers, etc. I have individual casserole dishes that I use to reheat things and find that I can just put them in the toaster oven for a few minutes. Sure, I'd like to have a microwave, but there again lack of space rules. It's all about choices.

A NOTE TO READERS . . . AND COOKS

Cookbooks, I've found, are never finished. After I decided this one had enough recipes and advice, I turned it over to editor Carol Roark and then to designer Amy Balamut. But I kept finding new recipes, new things to cook, new twists on old ideas, and, yes, cooking mistakes and even disasters. They're easy in a tiny kitchen.

I could have kept adding to this cookbook forever, until it was too thick to use easily and too expensive to buy. I had to quit somewhere. And yet I want to continue to share my recipes with you. I want to make this cookbook an ongoing project.

I am developing a blog for *Gourmet on a Hot Plate*. Places where I can post recipes and idea, and you can share your recipes, culinary triumphs, and occasional mistakes. If you'd like to be part of this conversation, please sign up for my newsletter by sending me your name, your city, and your email address at j.alter@tcu.edu.

In late October or early November, a new blog, "Gourmet on a Hot Plate," will be active and ready for your comments. The blog will make adventures in a tiny kitchen an ongoing project—I'll welcome comments, questions, recipes, and suggestions, and I'll try to offer new recipes. Let's explore tiny kitchen cooking together.

Let's keep on cooking!

Appetizers

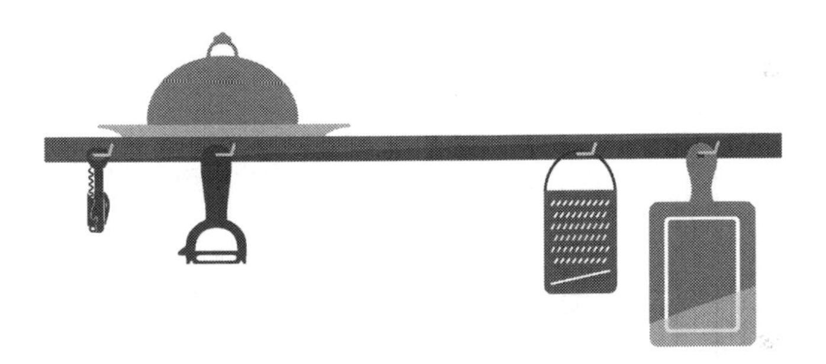

BRIE WITH TOPPING

INGREDIENTS:

6-inch brie.

½ c. brown sugar

½ tsp. cayenne

DIRECTIONS:

Slice away the rind on the upper side of the cheese but leave it intact on the sides or your brie will run all over the baking dish.

Top with a mixture of sugar, well mixed with ½ tsp. cayenne—you can make any amount to fit your brie. Just keep the proportions. I have done ¼ cup sugar with ¼ tsp. cayenne for a smaller round of brie, and 1 cup sugar to 1 tsp. cayenne for a really large brie.

Bake until cheese is soft and topping is melted—about 10 minutes in a 350° oven, but watch it closely.

Serve with crackers.

GOAT CHEESE LOG

This is quick, easy, and delicious. Warning: my dog once snatched a whole log off the coffee table and ate it. I expected middle-of-the-night gastric distress, but she must have a stomach of cast iron.

INGREDIENTS:

One log plain goat cheese

Wasabi paste

toasted sesame seeds

Soy sauce

DIRECTIONS:

Split the goat cheese horizontally and drizzle the bottom half with wasabi paste in sort of an "S" pattern, then put the other half of the log back in place. Roll in toasted sesame seeds (watch them carefully—I often have to toast them twice because I burn the first batch). Refrigerate. Just before serving, douse with soy.

IMITATION ESCARGOT

Quick and easy. I once made these for company and had them sitting in a basket on the counter, ready to serve. My children, then young, thought they were miniatures of the pecan rolls I sometimes made for breakfast and snitched a few. They got what for them was a rude awakening. For adults enjoying a pre-dinner appetizer, these are addictive.

INGREDIENTS:

1 pkg. crescent rolls

2 Tbsp. anchovy paste

2 Tbsp. butter or margarine, softened to room temperature

Dash of garlic powder

DIRECTIONS:

Flour a good-sized cutting board. Roll out the crescent dough as one piece, and pinch the perforations together. Mix butter, anchovy paste, and garlic powder. Spread evenly over dough rectangle. Roll up, starting with long end. Refrigerate roll briefly to make it easier to slice.

Slice cold dough roll into 1/2-inch pieces. Place pieces on ungreased cookie toaster-oven pan, and bake for 10–12 minutes at 350°. Rolls should be lightly browned.

Serve warm.

ONION TOAST STICKS

Onion soup mix recipes are ubiquitous, but here's one you may not have tried. It makes a lot.

INGREDIENTS:

½ cup onion butter*

12 slices good white bread

DIRECTIONS:

Cut crusts off bread. Spread butter on one side of each piece of bread, and then cut bread into strips.

Bake in preheated toaster oven on ungreased pan until strips are golden brown Serve warm.

*To make onion butter, mix 1 packet onion soup mix into two sticks (1/2 lb.) softened butter or margarine.

AMAZING CHEESE SPREAD

INGREDIENTS:

½ lb. cheese ends—those bits you have in the fridge and don't know what to do with

1 garlic clove

White wine as needed—start with ¼ cup and add more if necessary to make a creamy spread, but don't let it get runny

Several grinds of fresh black pepper

DIRECTIONS:

This actually comes straight from Jacques Pepin and is what he says his father used to do with cheese bits and ends. He called it fromage fort, appropriately, because it really is "strong cheese." It is a snap to make using a food processor. Much depends on the kinds of cheese you use. If you choose cheddars and/or fairly mild cheeses—like the Havarti I had left over the other day—your get one thing; add blue cheese to your fromage fort, and it changes the whole character.

Hint: If the cheese is really soft, cut it in small pieces; anything bordering on firm should be grated, to avoid straining your processor. Put it all in the processor and go for it.

AVOCADO DIP

Courtesy Subie Green

INGREDIENTS:

2 avocados, ripe

1/3 cup Greek yogurt, plain

1 cup cottage cheese

2 garlic cloves, pressed

2-3 diced green chilies, or 1 small can chopped

Salt and pepper to taste

Juice of ½ lemon

2 Tbsp. chopped mint (optional)

DIRECTIONS:

Peel avocados and cut meat into small cubes. Mix all ingredients together, stirring gently. Taste for lemon juice and add more if needed. Sprinkle with mint, if using.

CAESAR DIP

Love Caesar salad? This is for you.

INGREDIENTS:

1 cup mayonnaise

½ cup sour cream

½ cup grated Parmesan (not the stuff in a green can)

1 Tbsp. lemon juice

1 garlic clove, pressed

1 anchovy filet, mashed, or 1 tsp. anchovy paste (you can keep a tube of paste in the fridge and use small amounts without wasting an entire can).

DIRECTIONS:

Stir all the ingredients together.

Hint: Do not omit anchovy—it makes the dip, and you won't get a fishy taste.

CHEESE PLATTERS, CHARCUTERIES AND ANTIPASTO

I think of these as versions of the same dish. All three are easy to put together if you plan ahead and have the ingredients. A cheese platter maybe the easiest, but with the price of good cheese these days, it may not be the least expensive. Charcuterie is the traditional meat platter of France. Antipasto is traditionally the first course of a formal Italian dinner, but in this country, it has gone from the seated table to the happy hour coffee table. You often find the same ingredients on charcuterie and antipasto platters. The key to all three platters is variety in taste, texture, and eye appeal.

CHEESE PLATTERS

You can choose from four basic types of cheese: aged (cheddar, brie, gouda, goat, various types of Swiss); soft (camembert, Havarti, feta); firm: Manchego, Parmigiano, Pecorino; blue: (blue, gorgonzola, stilton). For a small gathering of perhaps four people, three choices, one each from three of the groups, are probably enough. Count on a third of a pound per person. Offer a choice of crusty breads and crackers. I'd put each cheese on a separate dish or board, so they don't "share" flavors, and be sure to put out a separate knife for each.

Refrigerate cheese until two or three hours before serving; bring to room temperature.

Possible accompaniments: honey, chutney, artichoke hearts.

[Note: a favorite treat a young friend recently introduced me to: put a bite of blue cheese on a cracker or slice of apple or pear and then drizzle just a drop or two of honey on it. Delicious! You can also spread a really thin layer of honey on a slice of feta and bake it briefly.]

CHARCUTERIE

Traditionally this is a platter of cold, cured or preserved meats. Once again, you want to mix texture and taste. Use one or more salamis, perhaps a hard and a soft; a pate or terrine; sausage; thinly sliced ham, possibly rolled for easier eating; prosciutto or its beef cousin bresaola. If you include a smoked meat, limit it to one. As one chef says, after a while all you taste is smoke.

HUMMUS

Who knew that you could make delicious hummus at home without dirtying twenty-five pots and doing lots of chopping and pressing and work? My version relies on an article in Christopher Kimball's *Milk Street Magazine*, May 2017.

INGREDIENTS:

8 oz. dry garbanzo beans (or chickpeas—whatever name your store recognizes)

½ cup reserved cooking liquid

2 Tbsp. salt, preferably kosher

1 tsp. additional salt

¼ tsp. baking soda

¼ cup tahini (sesame seed paste, resembles peanut butter)

1-1/2 Tbsp. lemon juice

1 Tbsp. good olive oil

1 Tbsp. parsley, finely chopped

½ tsp. cumin

½ tsp. paprika

DIRECTIONS:

Soak garbanzos overnight in ten cups water. Next day, drain and cover with 8 cups water. Add additional salt and baking soda. Bring to boil. Reduce heat to medium and cook about 45 minutes. You'll actually see the skins fall off the garbanzos. Drain, reserving ½ cup cooking liquid.

[Note: I know people who make hummus with canned garbanzos. I was trying to be a purist and cooked my own, but I'm sure canned are acceptable if you rinse them thoroughly. Trouble is, you don't get the saved cooking water specified above.]

Let beans sit until they are cool enough to put in food processor. Then add remaining ingredients including reserved cooking liquid; reserve the olive oil, parsley, cumin, and paprika. Blend a long time—at least two minutes. You can watch the color and texture change as the processor works.

Serve in a shallow dish. Make a well in the middle, and pour in olive oil. Decorate with cumin, paprika, and parsley.

MARINATED GOAT CHEESE

INGREDIENTS:

1 large log goat cheese (about 11 oz.)

1 Tbsp. fresh rosemary

1 Tbsp. grated lemon peel

1 garlic clove, pressed

½ tsp. coarse ground black pepper

1 cup olive oil

DIRECTIONS:

Cut cheese into 1/2 -inch slices and place in refrigerator container, preferably one where they can lie flat in a single layer. Add seasonings to the oil, and drizzle rounds with the oil. Refrigerate at least two days, no longer than five. Bring to room temperature to serve.

You can serve this with crackers as an appetizer or on a bed of lettuce or endive and tomatoes as a salad. Garnish with additional rosemary sprigs.

MUSHROOMS, CHEESE-STUFFED

This is a great cool-weather appetizer, another goodie from my mom. The amount below will feed two people three mushrooms each (they are rich) but can easily be varied to suit your needs.

INGREDIENTS:

Cheddar cheese, grated, about a cup

Sliced scallion

Pinch of dry mustard

Splash of Worcestershire

Just enough mayo to bind

Six good-sized mushrooms, caps intact, stems removed

DIRECTIONS:

Clean mushroom caps with a damp paper towel; discard stems.

Mix first five ingredients and stuff hollow caps.

Bake in a low oven (300-325°) until cheese melts and mushrooms appear cooked. The problem always is the cheese melts easily, but the mushroom remain raw. Keep an eye on them and use your best judgement. This spread is also good on toast and run under the broiler.

PICKLES AND HAM ROLLUPS

INGREDIENTS:

Ham slices—I prefer boiled or baked ham, not smoked, sliced a bit thicker than sandwich slice

Whipped cream cheese

Medium kosher dill pickles

DIRECTIONS:

This is the easiest appetizer ever. The recipe I found called for two thin slices of ham, but I found the second slice had nothing to hold it in place and peeled away. So I used a slightly thicker ham slice.

Slather a thin layer of cream cheese on the ham; put a pickle in the middle, and roll the slice. Cut into small rounds. One slice of ham will make four or five rounds, but in calculating remember that guests tend to eat a lot of these.

QUESO A LA COLIN

Favorite ever dish of my oldest son.

INGREDIENTS:

1 lb. hamburger

1 lb. ground sausage (your choice of mild, medium or hot)

1 16 oz. jar Pace picante sauce (again, mild, medium or hot—you choose)

1 can cream of mushroom soup

1 lb. Velveeta™ Original

DIRECTIONS:

Brown meat in skillet, breaking up the chunks. Put meat in a crock pot, add remaining ingredients and heat until cheese melts and ingredients are blended. Serve hot with tortilla chips. I used to put chips in the bottom of soup bowls, top them with this queso, and serve it to my kids as a one-dish meal.

RADISH SALSA

Ten years ago salsa was made with tomatoes, peppers, onion, and that was it. Now, everything becomes salsa. The first I ever made with something "daringly different" was a strawberry salsa. I made this radish one because my son-in-law, who is a bit vegetable challenged but getting better all the time, loves radishes. So easy.

INGREDIENTS:

6 large radishes, grated (use the large side of a box grater)

1 large cucumber, peeled, seeded, and finely chopped

½ cup chopped cilantro

1 garlic clove, pressed

1 Tbsp. lemon juice

¼ tsp. salt

DIRECTIONS:

Toss together. Chill before serving with chips.

REUBEN DIP

I have a son-in-law who wouldn't eat sauerkraut on a bet, but he loves this dip. I'm working up to trying a Reuben meatloaf on him. Meantime, the dip will do.

INGREDIENTS:

8 oz. cream cheese

½ cup mayonnaise

2 Tbsp. ketchup

1 Tbsp. bottled horseradish

1 Tbsp. dill relish

2 cups Swiss cheese, grated (about 8 oz.)

2 oz. deli corned beef, chopped

¼ cup sauerkraut, well drained

DIRECTIONS:

Mix cream cheese, ketchup, mayo, horseradish in bowl until well blended. Add remaining ingredients. Spray pie pan with oil, and spread mixture evenly over the bottom. Bake at 350 for 20 minutes. Serve with rye crackers or rye party rounds.

SALMON DIP

This is my favorite variation on the ubiquitous dip that everyone seems to make. It is easy and quick.

INGREDIENTS:

1 8 oz. pkg. cream cheese, softened to room temperature

½ cup sour cream

Splash of Worcestershire sauce

1 tsp. lemon juice

1 7 oz. can salmon, skin and bones removed, meat flaked

3 scallions, chopped

1 tsp. chopped parsley

1 tsp. dried dill weed (optional)

DIRECTIONS:

Blend first four ingredients in processor until smooth. Put in mixing bowl and fold in salmon, scallions, parsley, and dill (if using). Chill. Serve with crackers or baguette slices.

SARDINE/CHEESE SPREAD

INGREDIENTS:

1 can (3–4 oz.) boneless, skinless sardines, drained

1 cup cottage cheese

2 green onions, chopped (include tops)

1 Tbsp. lemon juice

2 tsp. Worcestershire sauce

¼ tsp. salt

Paprika

DIRECTIONS:

Blend all ingredients except onions and paprika in food processor. Reserve 2 tsp. chopped onion and stir the rest into the dip. Pack into dish and decorate with remaining onion and paprika.

SHERRY CHEESE PÂTÉ

INGREDIENTS:

6 oz. softened cream cheese (not whipped)

1 cup grated sharp cheddar

1 Tbsp. dry sherry

1/2 tsp. curry powder

1/4 tsp. salt

1 8 oz. jar mango chutney (or any chutney you prefer)

2 green onions, chopped

DIRECTIONS:

Mix cream cheese, cheddar, sherry, curry, and salt together, thoroughly. Spread the mixture on a serving plate. Chill. Spread the chutney on the top of the mixture and sprinkle green onions on the top. Serve with crackers.

SLICED EGGS WITH PARSLEY PESTO

I had this recipe, literally, for years before I read it and discovered you didn't scatter parsley over eggs and pour on oil. So I made it the right way and loved it. Thanks to artist Barbara Whitehead for giving it to me all those years ago.

INGREDIENTS:

2 cloves garlic, peeled

4 Tbsp. minced parsley

Salt and pepper

6 Tbsp. olive oil

5 hard-boiled eggs, thinly sliced crosswise

Grated carrot to garnish

DIRECTIONS:

Process first three ingredients; pour in oil gradually, processing until it forms a thick pesto.

Arrange eggs on a plate and sprinkle with salt. Pour on the pesto and decorate with carrot.

Refrigerate until well chilled, even overnight.

SOUTHWESTERN TUNA SALAD

A nice variation on tuna.

INGREDIENTS:

7½-oz. can albacore tuna

Juice of 1 lime (a good juicy one)

2 Tbsp. chopped cilantro

1 Tbsp. capers

¼ cup chopped celery

¼ cup chopped red onion

Pinch of cumin

Mayonnaise to bind

1 can chopped green chilies (Use your own judgment about canned chilies or a chopped jalapeño—I like the canned.)

DIRECTIONS:

Stir all the ingredients together.

Serve with crackers.

TUNA SPREAD

Tired of the ubiquitous smoked salmon dip? Here's a change that you can easily halve:

INGREDIENTS:

2 7-oz. cans good albacore tuna in water, flaked

8 oz. cream cheese, softened

1 green onion, chopped fine

Salt and pepper to taste

½ cup mayonnaise

2 Tbsp. hot sauce or to taste

2 Tbsp. fresh parsley

1 tsp. Worcestershire sauce

DIRECTIONS:

Blend all ingredients in food processor and chill at least six hours before serving. At the last minute, squeeze some lemon juice over it and stir in about ¼ cup fresh grated Parmesan. Serve with crackers or baguette slices.

Main Dishes

CHICKEN AND WILD RICE, EASY

Serves four. This is a great company dish. You can start it a couple of hours before company comes and let it bake unattended. EXCEPT if your toaster oven is like mine–it has a maximum of 30 minutes cooking time, so every half hour you have to tell it you want to keep cooking. It will beep when it goes off to remind you.

INGREDIENTS:

1 box Uncle Ben's Long Grain & Wild Rice (If you can find Original Recipe, so much the better; all I can find is Fast Cook.)

1 can cream of mushroom soup

1 can cream of celery soup

1 lb. chicken tenders

DIRECTIONS:

Thoroughly mix rice, seasoning packet, and two soups. Put in bottom of oven-proof casserole dish. Season chicken tenders with salt and pepper and lay on top of rice mixture. Cover tightly with aluminum foil and bake at 275°for two-and-a-half hours. Don't peek while it's cooking. Rice will be delicious, chicken tender and moist.

CHICKEN FINGERS WITH GARLIC BUTTER AND TOMATOES

My kids loved this when they were little. An oldie but goldie.

INGREDIENTS:

2 whole skinless, boneless chicken breasts, or 4 halves

Salt and pepper to taste

1 tsp. dried oregano

2 Tbsp. flour

2 Tbsp. butter

2 Tbsp. olive oil

4 plum tomatoes, skinned, seeded, and diced

1 Tbsp. chopped garlic cloves (do not use refrigerated pre-chopped garlic)

4 Tbsp. chopped fresh basil (optional)

2 Tbsp. fresh lime juice

DIRECTIONS:

Cut the breast halves in half crosswise and then into small strips. Put the salt, pepper, flour, and oregano in a small paper bag, and, a few at a time, add the chicken strips and shake to coat. No paper bag? Use a soup plate and roll the strips around in the mixture.

Heat oil and butter to hot in large skillet, place the chicken in a single layer for better browning, and cook until lightly browned. Lower heat and add garlic and tomatoes. Stir in well. Add lime juice and basil, if using. Cook, stirring well again.

Serve immediately. Should serve 6. You can cut the recipe in half easily.

CHICKEN POT PIE

Recipes for chicken pot pie are plentiful on the internet. I like this filling, because it uses cream cheese rather than sour cream and it incorporates grated cheddar. But without a real oven, the crust was problematic. I got this recipe from a Kraft ad for braiding crescent roll dough around the pie filling, but the braid clearly was not going to fit in my toaster oven.

I asked my daughter to bring some puff pastry, thinking I'd put the filling in individual dishes and top with the puff pastry; she brought puff pastry shells that had a clear warning: do not bake in a toaster-oven. I decided to cook the dish in one square CorningWare® dish and top it with crescent roll dough. That worked fine, except that I felt compelled to use every inch of the dough; it was too thick in some places and burned. Next time, for an 8 x 8" pan, I used half the dough and let it float on top. The rest can make individual rolls. The good news: three of us ate the whole thing in one sitting. My picky grandson had two helpings and ended up using his fresh strawberries to mop the remaining sauce up from the plate.

INGREDIENTS:

FILLING:
1 cup cooked chicken, diced, or a bit more

½ cup frozen petite peas

½ cup frozen corn kernels

½ cup cream of chicken soup

4 oz. cream cheese

½ cup cheddar cheese

TOPPING:
1 can of crescent rolls

DIRECTIONS:

Filling—Mix all together and put in greased 8 x 8" dish.

Topping—Roll out one tube of crescent roll dough. Set aside half for other use. In the remaining half, press the perforations together to make on seamless sheet of dough. Carefully lay it on the filling—it should almost but not quite cover it. Brush with egg wash (1 egg yolk and 1 Tbsp. water) if you wish.

Bake at 375° for 20 minutes. Crust should be golden, and filling should bubble.

CHICKEN THIGHS WITH SOY SAUCE AND LIME

This quick and easy recipe gives thighs the best flavor. I wouldn't try it with white meat, which is drier. Be sure to use bone-in, skin-on thighs. Serves four nicely.

INGREDIENTS:

1 to 2 thighs per person (6 to 8, total)

Salt and pepper

1 Tbsp. vegetable oil

Six scallions, finely chopped, divided

1 whole head garlic, halved crosswise

2 Tbsp. lime juice, plus 1 whole lime quartered

1 Tbsp. low sodium soy sauce

1 cup water

DIRECTIONS:

Salt and pepper both sides of the chicken to taste. Heat oil in large pot—most skillets are too shallow. Brown chicken, skin-side first, getting a good sear on both sides. Use tongs to flip carefully so that you don't disturb the skin.

Finely chop scallions. Add to the chicken in the pot, along with half head of garlic. Cook about five minutes—let onions brown but not the garlic. Add lime juice, soy sauce and cup of water to pot and let simmer. Cover the pot but leave the lid slightly ajar.

Cook until chicken is very tender, and liquid is reduced. Check it at 15 minutes and every five minutes thereafter. Remove half garlic head and squeeze cloves to add cooked garlic to chicken dish.

To serve: Place chicken on platter and scatter diced scallions over it. Microplane lime peel over chicken, and spoon sauce. Serve with lime wedges. Rice makes a nice accompaniment.

ROAST CHICKEN THIGHS AND CARROTS

This is another easy recipe, but I have a few cautions: the crust on the chicken is delicious but hard to keep on the meat when you eat. Let it sit just a bit before serving. Be sure to cut carrots into fairly small pieces so they get good and soft, the way roasted carrots should be.

INGREDIENTS:

¾ cup panko

4 Tbsp. butter, must be at room temperature, good and soft

¼ cup Dijon mustard

2 Tbsp. fresh thyme, or 2 tsp. dried

4 chicken thighs, seasoned with salt and pepper

2-4 carrots, scraped and cut into small chunks

DIRECTIONS:

Smear butter mixture on skin side of chicken; press chicken skin-side down into panko and coat as well as possible. Arrange carrot pieces around chicken, Season carrots with salt and pepper and then drizzle with olive oil.

Bale at 450° for 30 minutes. The crust should brown nicely and be crisp. Transfer to platter and pour juice over.

SMOTHERED CHICKEN

One of my gastronomic dislikes is a dry chicken breast. I like white meat, but I want some sauce with it, anything from gravy to mayonnaise in a chicken salad. This is a white meat chicken recipe that gives you both tender meat and a nice gravy. You can use boneless breasts but I always prefer bone-in, skin-on because they have more flavor. It is easy to remove the skin and carve around the bone.

INGREDIENTS:

Two chicken breasts or four halves

Salt and pepper

2 Tbsp. butter, more if needed

2 Tbsp. flour

1-1/2 cups chicken broth

¼ cup water

DIRECTIONS:

Salt and pepper chicken and brown in butter over medium heat. Add water to the skillet, cover and cook until chicken is cooked through. Remove lid and cook until liquid almost disappears. Remove chicken and keep warm.

If necessary, add more butter to skillet. Heat and stir in flour, making a roux. Gradually stir in broth until you have the consistency sauce you want. Season to taste with salt and pepper. Return chicken to skillet to heat through.
Nice served with mashed or boiled potatoes and a green salad.

If you like lots of sauce, double the butter, flour and broth—or serve it to two instead of four and only use two chicken breast pieces. You just want to change the proportion of chicken to sauce.

BEEF (HAMBURGER) STROGANOFF

Serves six; may be halved easily; makes good leftovers

Stroganoff is a classy dish, the kind of dinner you serve your sweetie, by candlelight with good red wine, on Valentine's Day . . . or a special family treat. But there have been two classic ways to do it: with beef tenderloin which cooks quickly and is tender, or with a cheaper cut, like beef tips, which requires all day in the crockpot. I do it with hamburger, and while the result is not as classy as tenderloin, it's darn good.

INGREDIENTS:

2 lbs. ground sirloin

½ cup flour

1 tsp. salt

½ tsp. pepper (I don't always use fresh ground—I like a finer grain in some dishes to avoid biting into a coarse piece of pepper)

4 Tbsp. butter, divided

½ cup finely diced onion

½ lb. mushrooms, sliced

2 cups beef stock

1 lb. egg noodles

1 cup sour cream

3 Tbsp. tomato paste

1 tsp. Worcestershire sauce

DIRECTIONS:

Brown ground meat in 2 Tbsp. butter; if necessary, brown in batches. Stir in flour, salt and pepper. Remove meat from skillet. Brown onion in remaining 2 Tbsp. butter (you may not need all the butter, if the ground meat leaves enough grease in the skillet). When onion is translucent, add mushrooms and sauté until nicely wilted. Add beef stock and bring to slight boil, cooking until sauce thickens. Remove the pan from your hot plate.

This is where you have to juggle when you have only one hot plate. Heat a large pot of salted water for noodles. When you're ten minutes away from serving, cook noodles and drain. Plop them right back into that warm pan and cover to maintain heat. Stir in a little butter or olive oil to keep the noodles from sticking to each other.

Mix sour cream, tomato paste (you know it comes in a refrigerator tube, don't you? You don't have to use a small can each time you need just a bit), and Worcestershire sauce. Return meat to burner and heat. Stir a spoonful of hot beef mixture into the sour cream, and then stir the whole thing back into the meat. DO NOT LET IT BOIL. If it boils, the cream will curdle. Stir to warm the sour cream mixture and mix thoroughly, and then dump it into the noodles. You may serve the two separately if you want, but the dinner stays warm better this way. Serve immediately.

All you need with this is a green salad.

Use leftover within two or three days and do not boil when reheating.

CHEESY, CREAMY BEEF NOODLE CASSEROLE

INGREDIENTS:

6 oz. egg noodles

2 lb. ground beef

1 medium onion, chopped

3 Tbsp. garlic

Salt and pepper to taste

Sliced mushrooms—optional

1 can each—cream of mushroom and cream of chicken soup

1 can corn, drained

1 cup grated cheddar (more of you wish)

1 sleeve buttery crackers (I use Ritz), crushed

½ stick butter (4 Tbsp.), melted

DIRECTIONS:

Cook egg noodles according to package directions and set aside. Rinse and swish with a little olive oil.

Brown beef with garlic, salt and pepper, and mushrooms. Drain. Add noodles to beef mixture along with soups and corn. Sprinkle with grated cheese. Mix crackers with melted butter; distribute evenly on top of the casserole. Bake 30 minutes uncovered at 350°. Enjoy! I never said it's good for your waistline.

NORWEGIAN HAMBURGERS

These really are meat cakes, but my family calls them hamburgers. The recipe comes from my oldest son's mother-in-law who grew up in Norway. I can't believe they had packaged gravy mixes when she was young—I think that's an American shortcut she has introduced!*

INGREDIENTS:

3–4 slices of onion

3 Tbsp. butter (do not use oil)

1½ lbs. extra-lean hamburger (extra-lean is important)

2 eggs

3 Tbsp. cornstarch or potato starch

½ tsp. pepper

Milk as needed, usually about ¼ cup

4-5 envelopes instant beef gravy mix, prepared as directed

2 beef bouillon cubes

DIRECTIONS:

Sauté onion in butter. Remove from skillet.

Mix hamburger, eggs, cornstarch, and pepper. Add milk as needed; start with ¼ cup Add more carefully only if needed, but DON'T let the meat mixture get soggy. The meat cakes will fall apart if too wet. Drop large spoonfuls in same skillet as you used for onions, flatten into a rough patty shape, and brown but do not cook thoroughly. Remove.

Make gravy in skillet, according to package directions. Add 2 bouillon cubes and stir to dissolve. When gravy thickens, return burgers and onions to pan and simmer for 45 to 60 minutes.

Serve with white rice, egg noodles, or boiled potatoes. Peas, beets, or green beans are nice with this.

**Note: I have since learned i misjudged her. They had a powdered beef product in WWII*

SHEPHERD'S PIE

Shepherd's pie is generally thought of as a meat dish with a mashed-potato topping. Some confusion exists between Shepherd's pie and Cottage pie. The former is an Irish dish and uses lamb; the latter is English and uses beef. But nobody's going to hold you to that distinction—use whichever you prefer. I sometimes like lamb as a variation. Some people make this with cubed meat, but I think it's just fine with ground meat. Here's an easy version that serves four.

INGREDIENTS:

1 lb. ground meat, beef or lamb

2 Tbsp. flour

4 cups frozen mixed vegetables

¾ cup beef broth

2 Tbsp. ketchup

1 lb. red potatoes

2 cloves garlic

¾ cup sour cream

1 cup grated sharp cheddar

Salt and pepper

DIRECTIONS:

Brown meat in skillet and pour off grease (if you use lamb, there will be a lot of grease). Stir in 2 Tbsp. flour, beef broth, ketchup, and vegetables. Set aside.

Quarter potatoes and boil, with garlic, until soft. Skin on or off is your choice. Rough mash in large bowl and add sour cream and cheddar. Salt and pepper to taste.

Spread meat mixture in a baking dish. Top with potatoes. Bake 20 minutes at 350° or until meat is bubbling and potatoes are lightly browned.

STEAK AND VEGGIES IN A SKILLET

For two.

INGREDIENTS:

¾ lb. New York strip steak, boneless

Salt and pepper

1 Tbsp. olive oil

3 garlic cloves—grate one, slice two

6 scallions, chopped

1 cup frozen petite pois (green peas, small)

1 small bunch asparagus—about 8 stalks, cut into pieces

FOR THE SAUCE:

1/3 cup Dijon mustard

1 Tbsp. red wine vinegar

1 tsp. honey

A pinch of cayenne or paprika, according to taste

½ cup olive oil

DIRECTIONS:

To make the sauce: Whisk together grated garlic, mustard, red wine vinegar, honey, and oil with 1 Tbsp. water. Set aside.

For steak: Pat the steak dry, season with salt and pepper, and rub with olive oil. Sauté on medium heat until medium rare, turning frequently to brown evenly. Set aside.

Add scallions and sliced garlic to skillet and cook until soft. Add peas with just enough water to cover the bottom of the pan. Cook, stirring and mashing slightly, for about five minutes. Add asparagus pieces, cooking another five minutes.

Slice steak and layer over vegetables in skillet. Drizzle with mustard sauce or serve sauce on the side. Serves two generously.

SAUTÉED LAMB CHOPS

I love lamb and find that those thick but small loin lamb chops are a perfect dinner for me. After reading a complicated recipe, I came up with a much-simplified version.

INGREDIENTS:

1 loin lamb chop per person

Salt and pepper

Olive oil

Butter

Anchovy paste

1 scallion per person, chopped

DIRECTIONS:

Season lamb chop(s) with salt and pepper. Brown and cook to desired doneness—I like mine on the rare side of medium rare. Remove from pan and keep warm under foil tent.

Add a dollop of butter for each chop to the pan. Sauté scallion until wilted but not browned. Add a dollop of anchovy paste (about 1 tsp.) for each person Stir to blend thoroughly. Pour over chop and serve immediately.

LAMB BURGERS WITH TZATZIKI SAUCE

INGREDIENTS:

FOR THE BURGERS:

1 lb. ground lamb

½ cup fresh white bread-crumbs

1 small onion, diced

2 Tbsp. chopped flat-leaf parsley

2 cloves garlic, minced

1 Tbsp. dried oregano

Salt and pepper to taste.

DIRECTIONS:

Season lamb with salt and pepper. Mix ingredients together thoroughly and shape into four patties. If you want small patties, this will easily make five.

Best if grilled, but you can pan fry.

Serve with tzatziki sauce (see recipe in condiments). Can serve as is or in pita pockets with lettuce and tomato.

PORK ROAST WITHOUT AN OVEN

A colleague served this one night, and it was delicious. I didn't believe him when he told me how he cooked it, so I tried it. Now it's a family favorite, perfect for the tiny kitchen without an oven. And it uses a cheap cut of meat. Can't beat that.

INGREDIENTS:

PORK ROAST:

2-1/2 lbs. Boston butt roast, untrimmed and cut into 1-inch cubes

2 cups water

2 Tbsp. salt

GARLIC SAUCE:

½ cup fresh lime juice

2 garlic cloves, pressed.

Salt and pepper—go easy on the salt, as the meat cooked in salted water, but I suggest at least a half tsp. pepper

DIRECTIONS:

Ask the butcher to cube the roast for you, if you have access to a butcher. Their idea of cubes is usually pretty big chunks, but it's a start. You just have to cube the cubes until you get something the size you want—about an inch.

Bring the water and salt to a boil. Add the cubed meat and reduce to a simmer. Cook for at least an hour and a quarter, until all the water evaporates. The meat will look unappetizingly white, but cook it longer, stirring occasionally, and the cubes will develop a nice brown crust.

Serve with garlic sauce and lime wedges.

NOTE: For a fancier version see the recipe for Carnitas on the next page.

CARNITAS

With a little more trouble, you can turn the Pork Roast recipe on the previous page into carnitas.

INGREDIENTS:

2-1/2 lbs. Boston butt roast, untrimmed and cut into 1-inch cubes

2 cups water

One good-sized onion, roughly chopped

6 strips orange zest (serve orange wedges as a side to the dinner)

5 garlic cloves, minced

½ tsp. crushed red pepper flakes

1 cinnamon stick

2 bay leaves

1-1/2 tsp. dried oregano

1-1/2 tsp. kosher salt

2 whole cloves

DIRECTIONS:

Ask the butcher to cube the roast for you, if you have access to a butcher. Their idea of cubes is usually pretty big chunks, but it's a start. You just have to cube the cubes until you get something the size you want—about an inch.

Bring the water and salt to a boil. Add the cubed meat, chopped onion, orange zest, garlic cloves, crushed red pepper flakes, cinnamon stick, bay leaves, oregano, and cloves to the water and reduce to a simmer. Cook for at least an hour and a quarter, until all the water evaporates. The meat will look unappetizingly white, but cook it longer, stirring occasionally, and the cubes will develop a nice brown crust.

Serve on tortillas with any or all of the following:

- Sour cream
- Chopped Cilantro
- Grated Monterrey Jack cheese
- Finely diced red onion
- Pico de Gallo

Brava! You have tacos de carnitas! Serve in tortillas or in pita pockets with lettuce and tomato.

SCALLOPS IN LEMON SAUCE

Serves two.

INGREDIENTS:

1 large lemon

3-4 large sea scallops per person

4 sliced mushrooms

Salt and pepper to taste

1 Tbsp. butter

¼ cup white wine

1 Tbsp. water

½ tsp. cornstarch

Optional: 1 Tbsp. minced fresh basil or parsley

DIRECTIONS:

Grate lemon peel and reserve ½ tsp. Also reserve 2 Tbsp. lemon juice.

Dissolve cornstarch in water.

Sprinkle scallops lightly with salt and pepper. Sauté mushrooms in butter over medium heat; when soft, remove from skillet and set aside. Sauté scallops until they are medium brown on either side—do not overcook or they will get rubbery. Remove and set aside.

Add wine and lemon juice to skillet. Heat and stir in cornstarch mixture. Cook stirring constantly until mixture is slightly thickened. Return mushrooms and scallops to skillet and keep it on a low heat. Sprinkle with basil or parsley and grated lemon peel.

Serve immediately, garnishing with grated lemon peel. Warning: once you start to cook the scallops, dinner is less than 5 minutes away, and this dish doesn't reheat or keep nicely.

SHRIMP VICTORIA

To my great dismay, I can no longer eat this. In my thirties I developed an allergy to shrimp. But if you want a dish that's showy for company—a bit rich—and quick and easy, you can't beat this. I haven't yet come up with an acceptable substitute for the shrimp for me, but y'all enjoy.

INGREDIENTS:

½ cup onion, diced

1 stick butter

2 lbs. shrimp

1 lb. mushrooms, sliced

2 Tbsp. flour

1 tsp. salt

Pinch of pepper

2 cups sour cream, more if needed

Rice or noodles

DIRECTIONS:

Sauté onion in butter until translucent. Add mushrooms and cook two minutes. Add shrimp and cook four minutes, stirring.

Sprinkle flour, salt, and pepper over mixture, stirring to incorporate thoroughly.

Just before serving, stir in sour cream. Don't heat but a minute, or the cream will curdle.

Serve over rice or noodles.

PAN FRIED TROUT FOR TWO

This recipe called for cooking the trout in an iron skillet in your fireplace. Showy, but not necessary. It comes out just as tasty if you cook it in a skillet on your hot plate.

INGREDIENTS:

¼ cup olive oil

1 clove garlic, sliced

2 anchovy filets

Salt to taste

Flour

1 large trout, fileted

DIRECTIONS:

Sauté garlic in oil. Add anchovy and stir until it is mushy. Season trout with salt and pepper and a light dusting of flour to keep it from sticking. Add trout to skillet, flesh side down. Cook over medium until lightly browned and the flesh is firm Be sure not to overcook as it dries out the fish. Better to give a little on the browning than to overcook. Split filet and place on two plates, working quickly. Pour oil from skillet over trout and serve.

TUNA CASSEROLE

Be assured this is not the tuna and noodle casserole from the sixties and seventies.

INGREDIENTS:

One cup white wine

Handful of herbs—thyme, rosemary, tarragon, oregano, black pepper, savory, parsley, whatever strikes your fancy, though I'd leave out cumin, chile powder, and related Mexican spices

Egg noodles—maybe 5 oz. or so

1 7-oz. can chunk albacore tuna

1 can cream of mushroom soup—not low fat

Vegetable of choice—I like frozen green peas; use however much you want

Dash of Worcestershire sauce

Salt and pepper to taste

Pinch of dry mustard, if you want

French fried onion rings or other crispy topping of your preference—buttered Ritz cracker crumbs are also good. Nobody said this is a Weight Watchers® recipe!

DIRECTIONS:

Boil wine and herbs hard until mixture turns black. Remove from heat and set aside.

Boil some egg noodles. Drain and rinse. Mix tuna, noodles, soup, wine mixture, vegetable and seasonings. Place in an 8" square baking dish, or one of a similar size that will fit in your toaster oven. Top with topping of choice and bake at 350° until casserole is bubbly, and topping is brown, usually for about 25–30 minutes. Honest, it's good! But then, I like almost anything with tuna.

TUNA FLORENTINE

Tuna and spinach are two of my favorite foods. This one, meant to be a good-sized casserole, is a bit of work but well worth it. Might be a good one to bake in two individual casseroles. I have cut the original recipe in half here, so feel free to double it and bake in batches or whatever works for you.

INGREDIENTS:

1 Tbsp. butter or as needed, divided use

½ half small onion or six scallions diced

1 10 oz. pkg. frozen chopped spinach (reserve cooking liquid)

Salt to taste

Milk as needed

A good pinch of ground nutmeg

1 7 oz. can oil-packed tuna, preferably olive oil

1-1/2 Tbsp. flour

Slight pinch of mace

½ cup grated Swiss cheese

1 Tbsp. Parmesan cheese grated

1 Tbsp. white wine

Topping:

¾ cup soft bread crumbs

1 Tbsp. Parmesan cheese

2 Tbsp. melted butter

DIRECTIONS:

Sauté onion in melted butter.

Cook spinach separately until tender; drain thoroughly, reserving cooking liquid. Add onion and butter, season with salt, pepper and nutmeg. Simmer briefly to blend flavors.

Add milk to spinach cooking liquid to make ¾ cup.

Drain and flake tuna, reserving oil. Put 1 Tbsp. reserved oil in skillet with ½ Tbsp., more or less, butter and heat to melt butter. Blend in flour, mace, and salt and pepper. Add spinach liquid/milk mixture and stir to create a smooth sauce. Remove from heat, add cheeses and wine. Heat again until smooth. Add tuna.

Place spinach in bottom of baking dish(es), top with tuna. Add topping, made by mixing melted butter, bread crumbs, and Parmesan thoroughly.

Bake, uncovered, at 350° until lightly browned, generally about 30 minutes. If using two small dishes, check your oven at 20 minutes and again at 30.

TUNA STUFFED ZUCCHINI

INGREDIENTS:

2 Zucchini

TUNA MIX:

Saved interior of zucchini, chopped

1 7 oz. can tuna

1 cup shredded cheddar

1/4 cup chopped celery

1 Tbsp. chopped parsley (about the extent of my current parsley crop)

1/3 cup sour cream

DIRECTIONS:

Boil zucchini until just soft. When cool enough to handle, split lengthwise and carefully hollow out. Add scooped out squash to stuffing mixture. Stuff into zucchini shells; top with more grated cheddar and bake or broil until cheese topping is lightly browned and filling is bubbly.

Skillet Suppers

Skillet Suppers - Eggs

EGGS

For a simple supper for one or two, never overlook eggs. They're delicious, nutritious, and offer so many opportunities for variation. I'm not sure to this day that I understand the frittata craze. Frittatas are either overcooked, open-face omelets or crustless quiches. I have easier things to do with eggs. Neither do I make omelets. I never learned that twist of the wrist, and why go to all that trouble when scrambled eggs have all the same flavors?

SCRAMBLED EGGS

Scrambled eggs offer plenty of opportunities for additions, but there's nothing wrong with just plain scrambled eggs, bacon and toast—breakfast for dinner. I belonged to a group that christened it brinner and used to have potluck brinner parties.

I have to make it plain: I like my eggs soft-scrambled. Some of my family cook them until they are hard little bits of concrete, but I like them soft and fluffy. One night recently, I layered cold-smoked salmon on a piece of well-buttered toast, scrambled my eggs with a bit of heavy cream, salt and pepper. A note here: I think it's important to whip the raw eggs vigorously so that you get a lot of air in them—that makes them fluffy.

When my eggs were barely set, I piled them on the toast, topped the whole thing with chopped chives, and ate it like an open-faced sandwich. Okay, in truth, I had to use knife and fork, but it was so good.

Later, I saw a recipe suggesting a schmear of avocado beneath the salmon would be good.

Not a fan of lox? Try prosciutto and caramelized onion, or a good salami. I once took a daughter-in-law to the local deli, where she ordered salami and eggs, expecting pieces of salami, maybe fried, on the side of her eggs. Nope. The salami was diced and incorporated into the eggs. You can do the same thing with lox. Or you can put in tomato and onion. My son-in-law regularly puts grated cheddar into eggs. A friend loves to scramble his eggs with rice leftover from a Mediterranean restaurant. Diced crisp bacon also wouldn't be a bad addition. I'm not a fan of peppers, but if you like them, they'd be good.

BAKED EGGS

I honestly never thought about baking eggs until I tried this recipe one night. For one. It was delicious.

INGREDIENTS:

1 half slice good sourdough bread

1 slice bacon, diced, cooked, and drained (reserve 1 tsp. grease to cook spinach)

A handful of baby spinach, cooked and drained

2 Tbsp. sharp cheddar cheese, grated

1 large egg

1 tsp. cream or milk

DIRECTIONS:

Grease a small ramekin well. Toast sourdough bread and butter both sides. Shape toast into ramekin until it forms a lining in bottom of dish.

Sauté bacon and drain, reserving 1 tsp. of grease to sauté the spinach. Cook spinach until just slightly wilted. Drain and cut into bite sizes pieces. Put spinach on toast; add cheese.

Carefully break egg on top of spinach, being sure to keep the yolk whole. Add salt and pepper and pour cream or milk over egg to keep it from drying out.

Bake at 350° for 12–14 minutes, until yolk is set but still runny. Before serving, top with bacon crumbles.

Again, the possibilities are endless. Substitute rice or hash browns for the bread. A bit of canned tomatoes might be good. Use crumbled sausage instead of bacon. Season with salsa. Flavor with herbs. I have had baked eggs on top of chicken livers and tomato—yum good. Top with bread crumbs. Think up your own combinations.

HARD-BOILED EGGS

One of my daughters buys pre-boiled and shelled eggs at the grocery, but I think that opens too many opportunities for contamination. I boil them at home. Start them in cold water to which you've added a splash of vinegar to keep them from leaching out of their shells during boiling. Boil gently for five minutes; remove from heat, cover, and let sit until water is room temperature. Refrigerate at that point.

Another hint: older eggs (two weeks or so) peel more easily when boiled.

I usually keep a couple of hard-boiled eggs in the refrigerator. You can slice and use for garnish or make the sliced eggs and pesto (see appetizers).

DEVILED EGGS

Deviled eggs are one of the world's delights. I like to mash the yolk with salt and pepper, add 1 sliced small green onion and just a tiny dab of Dijon mustard. Then add enough mayonnaise to bind—add carefully in tiny amounts, because there are few things worse than drippy, soupy deviled egg.

Of course, the variations are endless, both for things to incorporate with the yolk or top it with. Top the egg halves with pimiento or a snip of chives or a tiny twist of smoked salmon. Maybe 1/4 tsp. of caviar, should you have that handy, or a baby shrimp. Stir finely diced cooked bacon into the yolk or dice some of that smoked salmon. Add a couple of drops of Worcestershire sauce for a new taste.

BUFFALO EGGS

Buffalo eggs were new to me recently but are apparently common. Essentially, they're like deviled eggs but with different seasonings. Buffalo eggs are traditionally made with pickled eggs.

INGREDIENTS:

½ tsp. minced flat-leaf parsley

A drop of Tabasco or other hot sauce

Salt and pepper to taste; try using celery salt instead of Kosher

½ tsp. finely diced celery

Blue cheese to taste

Sprinkle with cayenne (optional)

DIRECTIONS:

Mix ingredients together.

PICKLED EGGS

In my experiment I found little difference in the eggs, except in the texture. I would suggest generally that it's not worth the trouble. But if you want to pickle eggs, here's an easy way:

INGREDIENTS:

(FOR TEN HARD-BOILED EGGS, PEELED)

1/3 cup water

1-1/2 cups white vinegar

3 Tbsp. pickling or table salt

1 tsp. whole black peppercorns

1 sweet onion (Vidalia or other) thinly sliced

DIRECTIONS:

Bring mixture to boil and let it boil briefly, just about a minute. Pack eggs and onion into a quart-sized jar. Let pickling mixture cool until it is just warm; pour over eggs. Seal the jar and refrigerator for at least 12 hours but no more than three months.

SHAKSHUKA, SORT OF

Shakshuka is a vegetarian dish of Tunisian origin that basically amounts to eggs poached in a seasoned tomato sauce. I used to cook an English version called Eggs in Purgatory that included potatoes and spinach in the sauce and was baked in the oven. This version of shakshuka is much easier and can be done on your hot plate. It includes anchovies, which you won't taste but, at the risk of repeating myself, it gives the dish a nice earthy taste. The problem here is to get the eggs done to the consistency that you and/or your guests like. This serves two but can easily be doubled—just use a bigger skillet.

INGREDIENTS:

2 Tbsp. olive oil

1 large garlic clove

2 anchovy filets (now figure out what to do with the rest of the can—or you can substitute 2 tsp. anchovy paste)

Pinch red pepper (I go really light with this)

1 14 oz. can diced tomatoes

Salt and pepper to taste—go slow with both as you'll have salt from the anchovies and pepper from that crushed red pepper.

1 tsp. dried basil (or a sprig of fresh if you have it)

4 eggs

Parmesan cheese

Baguette slices, garlic and olive oil

DIRECTIONS:

Slice garlic clove and dice anchovies. Put oil in skillet (use one with a tight-fitting lid), and sauté garlic and anchovies until garlic is slightly lightly browned and anchovies kind of melt into the oil—just a couple of minutes. Add tomatoes, salt, pepper, and basil. Simmer long and slow (about 20 minutes), mashing tomatoes occasionally. Don't let it dry out or reduce too much—if that happens, add a glug of white wine. What you want is a smooth, thick sauce.

When you're almost ready to serve, make four "pockets" in the sauce and drop an egg into each Put the lid on to steam the eggs and cook until they are desired doneness. Watch closely at this point.

Sprinkle with Parmesan cheese to serve. I find it best to serve this in bowls.

Good garlic toasts are a nice accompaniment. Toast baguette slices. Rub toasted slices with a cut garlic clove and drizzle with olive oil.

Nice, light supper.

PASTA

Pasta is a great dish for the hot-plate cook—it offers an easy way to entertain, and in this day, when pasta is no longer red sauce over spaghetti, you can experiment all you want. In fact, I find pasta a great way to use up leftovers. Whatever you choose to put in your sauce, pasta allows you to cook from scratch and to deal with individual foods in your final dish. As I keep repeating, so much better than dumping prepared red sauce over noodles. Though read on for a trick with prepared sauce.

One caution: most recipes call for cooking the pasta and, while it's cooking, making the sauce on another burner. If you only have one hot plate, you obviously can't do that. My trick is to cook the pasta, whatever shape and size you want, and rinse thoroughly in cold water when you get it to the doneness you want. Rinsing gets rid of most of that loose starch that makes cold pasta clump. Just to be sure, add the tiniest bit of olive oil to your pasta and stir to coat evenly. Sure, it will chill while you make the sauce, but when the sauce is ready, you can dump the pasta into the skillet and reheat.

An aside: I've discovered the advantages of serving pasta in soup plates. It makes everything so much easier.

Another aside: please use fresh grated Parmesan or Romano cheese—or Pecorino if you prefer. I don't buy grated cheese and don't use it. I wanted some Pecorino once and asked the cheese monger in an upscale store if he didn't carry it already grated. After all, I buy Parmesan and Romano grated fresh in his store. He explained he doesn't carry it because it comes with wood shavings mixed in to keep it from clumping. He grates the Parmesan and Romano and can testify they have no fillers. Lesson learned. And if it's true for a so-called gourmet cheese, don't even think about that pre-grated, pre-packaged cheddar in your daily grocery. I trust the freshly grated cheese from the cheese monger but not much else. I do keep frozen Parmesan or Romano cheese in the freezer.

LEFTOVERS IN PASTA (INVENT A BETTER NAME WHEN YOU SERVE IT)

One evening I was preparing to leave town the next day and wanted to use up what I could from the refrigerator. Prowling around, I found some good, thinly sliced ham left from a sandwich project, a stub of zucchini, and some asparagus that wouldn't last much longer. I had spinach fettucine in the cupboard—just the right amount.

I sliced the zucchini thin, julienned the ham, and cut the asparagus into bite-size pieces. I used salt and pepper generously on the vegetables. Then a dollop of butter—maybe 1/8 cup—went into the skillet, and I sautéed the vegetables a bit longer than the ham—they needed to cook, and the ham was precooked and very thin. When the vegetables were cooked, I added the ham and well-drained pasta to the skillet, stirred, and heated on low until thoroughly warm. Just before dishing, I gently blended in a good-sized dollop (heaping tablespoon) of sour cream and some Parmesan. Surprised myself both at how good it was and how much I ate.

This dish gave me vegetables, protein, and carbs and was sort of based on the principle of pasta primavera, and I think you could do it with any number of vegetables. Mushrooms would be good; so would cherry tomatoes halved, green peas, green beans—use your imagination. Prosciutto or bresaola would make a good protein, or you can always crumble crisp bacon in near the end of cooking. Use heavy cream or even half and half for the cream sauce or leave it a butter sauce and maybe squeeze some fresh lemon juice over it.

WITH A NOD TO JAMES BEARD

This is the easiest pasta I've ever made. I cut James Beard's original in half roughly. Toss about 4 oz. cooked linguine in 2 oz. melted butter in the skillet. Add half a cup of frozen baby peas—if you let them sit at room temperature for half an hour, no need to pre-cook. Roll 2 oz. prosciutto into a tight cylinder and slice. Toss it in the pan, stirring frequently to mix ingredients and make sure to separate the prosciutto strips. The meat is salty so be sparing if you add any salt—I found it needed just a pinch—but use pepper generously to taste. When everything is heated through, dish up to two pasta bowls and top with generous amounts of cheese—Pecorino, Romano, Parmesan, whatever, I particularly like the stronger flavor of Pecorino.

PASTA PRIMAVERA

Classic primavera, of course, is more than vegetables, butter and cheese. Here's a basic recipe you can use as a guide. Vary the proportions according to how many you're serving.

INGREDIENTS:

(FOR FOUR SERVINGS)

1 lb. linguini parboiled and drained

Broccoli flowerets

Small zucchini, sliced

½ lb. asparagus, cut into bites, with tough ends snapped off

Drain vegetables and set aside. Separately cook:

1 large clove garlic, minced

¼ cup olive oil

¼ cup chopped fresh basil, or 1 tsp. dried and crumbled

½ lb. mushrooms sliced

½ cup frozen petite green peas

¼ cup chopped parsley

1 tsp. salt

½ tsp. black pepper (use fine ground, not coarse, so nobody bites down on a pepper corn)

FOR THE SAUCE:

¼ cup butter

¾ cup heavy cream

DIRECTIONS:

Drain vegetables and set aside.

Sauté garlic and basil in oil, a minute or two; add mushrooms and sauté until they are cooked. Stir in the green peas, parsley, salt, black pepper.

Cook a minute or so. Add broccoli, zucchini, and asparagus; serve over linguini.

You can quit there, or you can use a separate large skillet to make the sauce.

PASTA WITH ASPARAGUS AND SMOKED SALMON

Serves two.

INGREDIENTS:

¾ lb. fettucine (I prefer spinach), cooked and drained

½ lb. asparagus

1 Tbsp. butter

½ Tbsp. minced shallots

1 cup heavy cream

4 oz. hot-smoked salmon, sliced ¼ inch chunks,

Salt and pepper to taste

1 tsp. fresh lemon juice

2 Tbsp. minced fresh dill (optional)

DIRECTIONS:

Steam asparagus until crisp-tender; drain and run under cold water to stop cooking.

In skillet, melt butter and sauté shallots. Add cream and simmer to thicken the sauce a bit.

Remove skillet from hot plate and add asparagus, salmon, lemon juice, salt and pepper. Stir in pasta and heat through. Serve, decorated with dill.

PASTA WITH BREAD CRUMBS AND ANCHOVIES

Throughout these pages I've repeated more than once that you should cook with anchovies, even if some people don't like them. They'll never know, and they add an earthy taste. That is not the case with this recipe. Only serve it if you like anchovies a lot—the taste is strong.

INGREDIENTS:

¼ cup good olive oil

1 garlic clove, peeled and halved

Pinch of red pepper flakes

1 can flat anchovy fillets, drained, rinsed and patted dry

¼ lb. spaghetti or fettucine, cooked according to package directions; reserve 1 Tbsp. cooking water

1 Tbsp. chopped parsley

¾ cup sautéed bread crumbs (see directions in Cooking Hints)

DIRECTIONS:

Sauté garlic in olive oil until garlic is golden. Remove garlic clove. Add pepper and anchovies, and cook about a minute over low heat, mashing the anchovies until they make a paste.

Cook spaghetti in boiling water. Before draining, add 1 Tbsp. of the pasta water to the anchovy mixture.

Toss drained pasta in skillet with sauce, distributing evenly. Sprinkle with parsley and breadcrumbs. Serve immediately.

TOMATO SAUCE

Want traditional tomato sauce? Here's one that simmers a long time to get that rich flavor. Serves four.

INGREDIENTS:

2 cups whole canned tomatoes, in their juices (San Marzano is the best brand)

8 Tbsp. (1 stick) butter (no substitutes, definitely not margarine)

1 onion, peeled, cut in half

Salt

DIRECTIONS:

Dump tomatoes into saucepan with juice, add the butter and set the onion halves down in sauce. Simmer, uncovered, stirring occasionally, for about an hour. During cooking, mash any big lumps with a wooden spoon. Remove onion. Salt to taste. You may want to add some Italian seasonings, such as basil, or you may choose to be a purist with the tomato flavor rich and strong.

You can serve this as is over a heavy pasta, such as rigatoni, or you can add crumbled, browned Italian sausage (hot or mild).

Top with Parmesan to serve.

SPAGHETTI SAUCE

Thanks to my friend Carol Roark for this traditional recipe updated for today's modern appetites. Carol's mother got the recipe from a woman living in Rome during the 1950s. It originally called for lots of ground beef, but Carol uses half the amount of meat and prefers ground turkey. This recipe can easily be doubled if your pot or slow cooker is big enough.

INGREDIENTS:

1 medium onion, chopped

2 cloves garlic, pressed

1 lb ground beef

2 Tbsp. olive oil

1 6 oz. can tomato paste

1 14.5 oz. can diced tomatoes

1 14.5 oz. can tomato puree

½ tsp. each sage, rosemary, oregano, thyme, savory, marjoram, and basil

Pinch of sugar

Salt and pepper

DIRECTIONS:

Cook the onions and garlic in olive oil until onions are slightly softened. Brown the meat. Add spices, salt, pepper and sugar. Add tomato paste, puree and diced tomatoes and stir well. Simmer on low heat for about 3 hours or in a slow cooker for 6 hours. Serve with your favorite pasta and fresh grated Parmesan.

FETTUCINE ALFREDO

This classic but elegant standby isn't as difficult as you may think. But it is rich.

INGREDIENTS:

2 Tbsp. butter

1 garlic clove, finely chopped

1-1/2 cups heavy cream

1 egg yolk

1 lb. fettucine

Parmigiano Reggiano cheese, grated

Freshly ground black pepper

DIRECTIONS:

Make the sauce first. Melt butter in large skillet. Add garlic and sauté until fragrant. Whisk cream and egg yolk in separate bowl until very well blended and then pour into the skillet. Lower the heat and stir constantly to keep egg from scrambling (scrambled egg on pasta is not a good thing). Cook until hot but do not let it boil. Remove skillet from hot plate.

Bring 6 quarters water to a boil. Add 2 Tbsp. salt. Cook fettucine until it floats to the top. Test for doneness. Drain in colander, saving a bit of the cooking water.

Return skillet with sauce to low heat and dump in the pasta. Add cheese, and cook, stirring, until cream is mostly absorbed. Season with salt and pepper. If dish gets too dry, cautiously add a bit of the reserved cooking water.

QUICK SPAGHETTI WITH ANCHOVY/ TOMATO SAUCE

Serves two.

INGREDIENTS:

1 can (14.5 oz.) diced tomatoes

1.5 Tbsp. olive oil

half a small onion, chopped fine

a garlic clove, pressed

7-8 anchovy filets (about one can, though you can use anchovy paste—1 tsp. equals a filet)

fresh basil leaves, chopped

Salt and pepper

DIRECTIONS:

Enough cooked linguine for two—I have one of those things with holes of graduated sizes—you stick some pasta through the hole for two and it tells you if you have enough or not.

CARBONARA WITH ANCHOVIES

This classic but elegant standby isn't as difficult as you may think. But it is rich. Serves four (or three who really like pasta and anchovies).

INGREDIENTS:

12 oz. linguine

1/4 cup olive oil

One sliced garlic clove

1 2-oz. can flat anchovies, drained and chopped

Pinch of red pepper (optional)

1/2 tsp. grated lemon zest

1 Tbsp. chopped oregano (it grows in a planter box on my porch)

1/4 cup chopped Italian parsley

2 large egg yolks

salt and pepper to taste

Grated fresh Parmesan cheese

DIRECTIONS:

Cook pasta and drain but keep ½ cup of the cooking water. Heat oil in skillet with garlic and anchovies and cook until anchovies come apart. Add pepper (if using), lemon zest, oregano and parsley. Add pasta, toss to coat, and remove from heat.

Separately whisk egg yolks with reserved pasta water; add to pasta and return to stove, cooking over low heat and tossing until pasta is coated in a creamy sauce—probably no more than a minute. Season with salt and pepper and serve with Parmesan.

POLENTA

Polenta began to appear on menus several years ago. Sometimes it's a nice substitute for potatoes or noodles or rice. And it's easier than you think. The Italians have known that for a long time.

INGREDIENTS:

½ tsp. salt

1-1/2 cups corn meal, yellow or white

2 cups cold water

2-1/2 cups boiling water.

DIRECTIONS:

Use a deep saucepan for this, as the cornmeal bubbles and spits as it cooks.

Put salt in 2-1/2 cups water and bring to a boil. Separately, whisk cornmeal into two cups ***cold*** water. Stir that mixture into the boiling water and bring it to a boil again, stirring. Reduce heat and simmer for 20 minutes. When cooked, polenta should have a thick but creamy texture. Dish it out onto a well-buttered single-layer cake pan, so that you can serve it in wedges. Let it sit to firm up.

At this point, use your imagination. I have stirred one cup cooked corn kernels into the mixture as it cooks, then topped the firm polenta with cheese and run it under the broiler. Serve in wedges.

You can also cover it with a sauce, perhaps you favorite marinara sauce. Or here's a mushroom sauce that's good.

MUSHROOM SAUCE FOR POLENTA

INGREDIENTS:

6 cups mushrooms, sliced

1 Tbsp. olive oil

1 medium onion, diced

2 cloves garlic, mashed

½ cup dry red wine

2 cups chicken stock

1 Tbsp. tomato paste

½ tsp. dried thyme

¼ tsp. dried rosemary

1 Tbsp. fresh parsley

1 tsp. lemon juice

Salt and pepper to taste

DIRECTIONS:

Sauté onions and garlic in olive oil until translucent. Add mushrooms and cook until soft. Add wine and bring to boil. Add stock, tomato paste, thyme and rosemary. Cook 20 minutes. Take a cupful of mushrooms out of sauce and puree in processor, then return to sauce. Stir in lemon juice, salt and pepper. If sauce is too thick, cautiously add chicken stock.

CREAMED TUNA OR CHICKEN

Sometimes I get a longing for comfort food, and creamed tuna or chicken on toast does it. Don't scoff! It's a simple dish to make, much like the creamed chipped beef, but with the addition of celery and onion. It is delicious when you feel like a gourmet indulgence.

INGREDIENTS:

1 Tbsp. butter

1 stalk celery, diced

3 scallions diced

1 Tbsp. flour

¼ cup white wine

Milk as needed

Salt and pepper to taste

1 7 oz. can water-packed albacore tuna, broken into small chunks, or 1 cup diced chicken

Creative optional additions:

A big dollop of sour cream

½ cup grated cheddar

DIRECTIONS:

Melt butter in skillet, and sauté celery and onion. Sprinkle with flour and stir to make smooth paste. Slowly stir in wine, and blend until smooth. Add small amounts of milk until sauce is consistency you want. Season with salt and pepper and then add tuna or chicken. At this point, either sour cream or cheddar make nice additions.

Serve hot over toast, a baked potato, rice, chow mein noodles, or whatever strikes your fancy.

SALMON CAKES

One of my favorite dishes remembered from childhood. And leftovers make the best cold sandwiches—with rye bread and mayo. There are many ways to make patties (if you're fancy, you can call them croquettes). Pretty much the same principles apply to chicken and tuna; ham is a bit different but worth trying.

Some recipes call for mashed potatoes as the binding agents; for a gluten-free friend, I've made them with almond flour; other recipes call for bread crumbs, and in that case the dried Progresso or similar brands work best. I have a friend who made them with rice, but I wouldn't advise that. My mom insisted on using finely ground saltine cracker crumbs, and Mom always knows best. Just whir them in the blender—do enough to hold the cakes together plus a bit to roll them in before sautéing. Mom shaped them into logs, but I find patties easier—difficult to brown all sides of a log equally.

INGREDIENTS:

15-oz. can pink salmon, bones, skin and all (it's good for you, and you'll never know it's there)

1 cup cracker crumbs (see note above)

Two or three scallions, thinly sliced

One stalk celery, chopped fine

2 eggs

Salt and pepper to taste

DIRECTIONS:

Mix above ingredients; best way to do it is to wash your hands and dig in; don't use blender or mixer. Shape into patties—should make about six. Coat patties in more cracker crumbs if you wish.

Sauté in vegetable oil over medium heat. If you've coated with crackers crumbs, they will burn easily. Remember the fish is already cooked. You're going for heat and a nice, brown crust.

Serve with lots of lemon or, should you desire, ketchup (probably a travesty). A good salad is nice with this, or you can serve them in burger buns.

See note above about leftovers. The leftover cakes will freeze nicely.

HAM PATTIES

I did not grow up with these, did not even eat one until recently, but I loved it. And really, they're easier than salmon patties, though I remain loyal to those.

INGREDIENTS:

1 egg, lightly beaten

2 Tbsp. pickle relish (I use dill, but the original recipe calls for sweet—your choice)

8 Tbsp. finely ground saltine crackers crumbs

1-1/2 tsp. Dijon mustard

10 oz. fully cooked ham, coarsely ground

3 Tbsp. butter, for frying

DIRECTIONS:

Mix everything but the butter thoroughly, being sure not to leave any stray bits of ham or cracker crumbs in the bottom of the bowl. If mixture is too thick, add just a bit of milk cautiously. Do NOT let it get soggy. Shape into six patties.

Fry in butter until just brown on each side. Serve hot. Or eat cold the next day.

SAUTÉED HAMBURGERS

These are a bit more work than just throwing a meat pattie into the frying pan, but they are well worth it. Note: Hate to open a can of tomato paste, tiny as they are, for just one Tbsp.? Look at your grocery for tomato paste in a tube. It will keep in refrigerator for some time (check expiration date).

INGREDIENTS:

FOR THE HAMBURGERS:

2 lbs. fresh ground lean beef

½ tsp. kosher salt

½ tsp. ground black pepper

4 Tbsp. heavy cream

Olive oil

FOR THE SAUCE:

2 Tbsp. scallions, minced (reserve green parts)

¼ cup wine, red or white as you prefer but use a dry wine

½ cup heavy cream

1 Tbsp. tomato paste

DIRECTIONS:

To make the hamburgers:
Mix the ingredients, using a fork to fluff the meat and keep it from getting packed too hard. Shape into four patties—they will be generous in size. Cover frying pan with a thin film of olive oil and cook burgers to desired doneness. Remove to a hot platter and tent with aluminum foil. Set in low oven—200°

To make the Sauce:
Remove all fat from pan except 1 Tbsp. (if burned, wipe skillet with paper towel to avoid burned taste). Sauté scallions briefly; add wine and bring to boil, scraping up any browned bits of meat. Reduce wine slightly. Stir in cream and tomato paste and boil until sauce thickens a bit—it won't get really thick.

Pour sauce over patties, decorate with reserved green onion tops, and serve immediately.

Vegetable Side Dishes

Vegetable Side Dishes

CHRISTIAN'S GREEN BEANS

INGREDIENTS:

4 slices bacon, cooked crisp and crumbled, or diced before cooking—reserve the grease

3 chopped scallions

2 large cans of green beans, sliced but not French cut

Generous splash of cider vinegar

DIRECTIONS:

Cook bacon and remove from skillet; sauté sliced green onions in reserved grease; add green beans; splash vinegar over all in skillet; toss and add crumbled bacon. Serve warm.

CORN, SPINACH, BACON & SCALLIONS IN A SKILLET

INGREDIENTS:

4 slices of bacon, diced

1 Tbsp. butter

1 shallot

2 cups corn kernels, (about 2 ears, cooked and cut from cob or about half a bag of frozen if necessary; fresh is best)

1 small summer squash diced

1 or 2 carrots, parboiled and sliced

Salt and pepper

2 or 3 scallions, thinly sliced

4 cups shredded spinach

DIRECTIONS:

Sauté bacon pieces until crisp; drain on paper towels and pour off grease, leaving 1 tsp. in the skillet.

Melt butter and sauté shallot; when it is soft, add remaining vegetables, except spinach—stir everything together, season with salt and pepper to taste, cover and cook over medium to low heat until squash is tender. Add spinach, cooking to wilt. Return bacon to pan and serve warm.

GERMAN POTATO SALAD

INGREDIENTS:

3-4 slices bacon, fried and crumbled; reserve grease

3 stalks celery, chopped

4 green onions, chopped

1 heaping Tbsp. flour

½ cup each water and vinegar

1 Tbsp. prepared mustard

2 cans sliced white potatoes

Parsley, for garnish

DIRECTIONS:

(The original recipe called for fresh cooked potatoes, of course, but this is one of the few places where I think canned does just fine and is actually better—they don't crumble like fresh-cooked potatoes.)

Hot dogs are optional: if you want to make this a one-dish meal, add 1 hot dog per person, brand of your choice (I like Hebrew National but often use Oscar Mayer Selects all-chicken franks these days—shhh, don't tell! They don't have a lot of other ingredients like preservatives—pure chicken breast).

Boil or grill the hot dogs (grilled is better). Fry the bacon and drain on paper towels; if there's too much grease in the skillet, drain some, but you want about 2 Tbsp. to cook this. Sauté celery and green onions in bacon grease. Add flour and stir. Add water and vinegar, a bit at a time, stirring—more of each as needed until sauce is a good consistency. Add mustard. Add potatoes. Crumble bacon and stir in. Cut hot dogs into chunks and mix in (traditional hot dogs make a more colorful dish than chicken, and as my mom always said, "Food is half eaten with the eyes.") Sprinkle with parsley just before serving.

SOUTHWESTERN BAKED POTATOES

Make these with medium-sized red potatoes, not big baking potatoes. They're so good, you'll wish for two.

INGREDIENTS:

Six red potatoes, medium to large

½ cup shredded cheddar

2 Tbsp. sour cream

1 Tbsp. melted butter

2 Tbsp. buttermilk

Salt and pepper

1 4-oz. can chopped green chilies

DIRECTIONS:

Scrub potatoes, cut a bit off the bottom so they'll sit flat, rub with oil, and bake at 350° until tender.

When potatoes cool enough to handle, scoop out the insides (carefully) and mash with remaining ingredients. Carefully stuff mixture back into the potatoes and bake until bubbly.

VEGETARIAN STUFFED ZUCCHINI

INGREDIENTS:

1 zucchini (serves two)

Celery, diced

Red onion, diced

1 Tbsp. sour cream

Grated cheddar

Grated Parmesan, fresh, please, not from the green shaker

Bacon (optional)

DIRECTIONS:

Halve the zucchini lengthwise and scoop out the center part. Dice scooped-out squash and mix with celery, red onion, sour cream, and grated cheddar. Stuff into zucchini shells. Top with Parmesan and bake 45 minutes at 350° or a bit less.

If adding bacon, fry it first, and stir into stuffing mixture just before baking.

Light Meals

ASPARAGUS WITH CHEESE FOR TWO

INGREDIENTS:

2 slices sourdough bread, not thickly sliced (Texas toast would, I decided, be too much bread and might get soggy in the middle.)

Melted butter

Shredded cheese, enough to cover both slices of bread—I'd use cheddar or, as I did the other night, the Jack/Colby combination

1 scallion, sliced

Pinch cayenne

Quick splash Worcestershire sauce

1/8 tsp. dry mustard

Mayonnaise

Four or five slices asparagus per person, halved lengthwise

Sliced cheese (the real thing, please, not "American sliced")

DIRECTIONS:

Mix shredded cheese with scallion, cayenne, Worcestershire sauce, and mustard. Add just enough mayo to bind. Set aside.

Melt about 2 Tbsp. butter and brush both sides of bread. Place on lightly greased cookie sheet and broil, watching closely and using tongs to turn. Remove from oven but leave broiler on.

Spread cheese mixture on toast; top with asparagus and sliced cheese. Broil until cheese is bubbly and just a bit brown.

BEEF FINGERS

I fed these to my kids all through school, and they ate heartily. I have no idea where I got the original recipe.

INGREDIENTS:

Beef cutlet—one per person

Salt and pepper

Flour

Vegetable oil for frying

Lemon juice

DIRECTIONS:

Cut beef into "fingers" about a half-inch to an inch wide. This is easier if the meat is slightly frozen. Salt and pepper thoroughly. Put fingers in a baggie or brown paper lunch bag, add enough flour to coat thoroughly. Shake the bag heartily, holding it closed so you don't get flour all over the kitchen.

Remove "fingers" one at a time, shaking off excess flour.

Heat oil in skillet to medium hot. Fry fingers in a single layer, leaving undisturbed long enough to develop a good crust. Turn and try for crust on the second side—never as easy.

Remove from heat and squeeze lemon juice over. Serve immediately.

BLUE CHEESE AND SALAD ON TOAST

A friend, who happens to be both a chef and a former student, was coming for lunch. I read through recipes and scoured my mind for something worthy to fix. You can't, I thought, fix tuna salad for a chef. This proved to be a hit.

INGREDIENTS:

2 slices good white bread, like a sourdough if the crust isn't too tough

Butter

4 oz. creamy blue cheese, sliced—I used Point Reyes

1 cup shaved celery (use your mandolin or just slice very thin)

2 scallions, sliced thin—including tops

1 large clove garlic

Olive oil

Lemon juice

Kosher salt

Black pepper

DIRECTIONS:

Toast the bread and spread with thin layer of butter.

Make a salad of celery, onion, olive oil, lemon juice, salt, and pepper.

Top toast with the sliced blue cheese (remember it's a strong flavor, so don't overdo); Top each toast and cheese with the salad. Microplane (you do have one, don't you?) the garlic over, and serve.

Serves 2. Nice in the summer, accompanied by fresh fruit, for a light lunch.

CHICKEN LOAF

Thanks to the late Carolyn Burk for this recipe. Half my family liked it; half didn't (I can't remember who does and who doesn't). I appreciate its pure, good chicken flavor. Nice to serve, with mayonnaise, as the centerpiece of a ladies' luncheon.

INGREDIENTS:

1 chicken hen or 2 fryers

1 cylinder saltine crackers

2 envelopes unflavored gelatin

2 cubes chicken bouillon

DIRECTIONS:

Stew chicken until cooked thoroughly. (You can't use rotisserie chicken for this, because you need the broth and you don't need all those seasonings—remember, you want pure chicken.) Add bouillon cubes to give the stock more flavor. Reserve the stock. Cool chicken and pull meat off bones. (If time permits I chill it thoroughly, so I can skim the fat off the top of the broth.) Chop finely. (Carolyn did it with scissors, but I use the food processor, being careful not to over-process.) Grind one cylinder of saltines in food processor and add to chicken. Soften gelatin in ½ cup of reserved stock. Add to chicken along with enough stock to bind it together—it should be moist but not soupy. Pack into a loaf pan. Cover with clear wrap, put another loaf pan on top, and weigh it down with canned goods. Refrigerate overnight.

It's hard to slice, because it crumbles, so take care. This will freeze but will not keep long after defrosting.

CHICKEN PAN BAGNAT

INGREDIENTS:

Rotisserie grilled chicken

Round loaf of artisan bread

¼ Tbsp. lemon juice

2 Tbsp. anchovy paste

Capers

1 garlic clove, pressed

2 sliced tomatoes

Sliced red onion to taste

Romaine lettuce leaves

DIRECTIONS:

Slice the bread in half horizontally and pull out all the bready insides; discard or freeze to use for bread crumbs, etc.

Drizzle anchovy/lemon sauce over top and bottom of bread.

Line bottom with capers, drained.

Slice chicken into slivers and put on bottom. Top with remaining ingredients.

Put the top on and smash it down with your hands to flatten. Wrap in foil and put in fridge overnight, weighted down by heavy skillet or canned goods—I used a lighter skillet and two cans of green beans. Cut into wedges and serve.

CHICKEN CAESAR SALAD

I like a good old-fashioned chicken or tuna salad, with the meat, maybe some celery and a scallion diced up and finished with a good dressing, almost always mayonnaise-based. Yet today in most restaurants if you were to order Chicken Caesar salad, you'd get a Caesar salad with slices of grilled chicken laid across the top. This one's different, but I bet you could use the dressing on good albacore tuna as well as on chicken.

INGREDIENTS:

3 cups finely diced cooked chicken

1 large stalk celery, finely diced

1 large scallion, finely diced

2 oil-packed anchovy filets, drained on paper towel

1 garlic clove

1 Tbsp. fresh lemon juice

1 Tbsp. cider vinegar

1 tsp. Dijon mustard

½ tsp. Worcestershire sauce

¼ tsp. each salt and finely ground black pepper

½ cup extra virgin olive oil

½ cup Parmesan cheese

DIRECTIONS:

Mix chicken, celery and scallion in large bowl. Place anchovy, garlic, lemon juice, vinegar, mustard, Worcestershire sauce, salt and pepper in processor and combine until smooth. Stir in Parmesan and pour dressing over chicken mixture and chill.

This can be served as part of a salad plate, attractively arranged on a lettuce leaf, or in a sandwich on French bread or a mini-baguette. If serving as a sandwich spread, split bread and spread with mayonnaise into which you've blended a bit of garlic powder. Broil before making sandwiches.

CHICKEN ROLLS

INGREDIENTS:

6 oz. cooked, chopped chicken

4 oz. cream cheese, softened

½ cup chopped mushrooms

2 Tbsp. sliced green onions

1 pkg. 8 crescent rolls

1 Tbsp. melted butter

DIRECTIONS:

Mix together chicken, cream cheese, mushrooms, and onions. Roll out crescent rolls to create four rectangles and pinch diagonal perforations on each rectangle together. Put equal portions of chicken mixture in the center of each of the four rectangles. Pull the dough up and over and pinch closed. Drizzle with melted butter and sprinkle with crushed croutons. Bake 12–15 minutes in a preheated 375° oven. If they start to get too brown, cover loosely with foil the last five minutes.

CURRIED CHICKEN SALAD

This is a go-to favorite, always good for lunch or a light supper for guests.

INGREDIENTS:

1 cooked chicken breast (rotisserie chicken is fine)

½ cup chopped celery

Vinaigrette of your choice (I like Newman's Own Vinaigrette)

½ tsp. curry powder or to taste

Enough mayonnaise to just bind the salad together Don't make it soupy.

TOPPING:

1 cup grated cheddar cheese

1 cup crushed potato chips

DIRECTIONS:

The tricky thing here is to use a refrigerator-to-oven dish. Do you have CorningWare®? Perfect. Otherwise, use a metal cake or pie pan. Chill the salad thoroughly. When ready to serve, sprinkle chips and then cheddar over it, and run under broiler just until cheese melts. Watch it carefully. Burnt potato chips are not a great addition.

EGG SALAD WITH CURRY

This egg salad offers a little variation on the standard formula and makes good sandwiches. Caution: it gets runny, as in watery, so use liquid sparingly and prepare to drain.

INGREDIENTS:

4 hard-boiled eggs, peeled

1 tsp. plain yogurt

½ tsp. olive oil

1 tsp. lemon juice

Sprinkle of cayenne to taste—you want a bit of sharpness to add zing, but not enough to make it spicy

¼ tsp. white wine vinegar

¼ tsp. curry powder or to taste

Salt to taste—be sparing; better to start small and add again than to over salt at first

DIRECTIONS:

Discard yolks of three eggs. Chop whites plus remaining whole egg until lightly mashed (do not use food processor). Add remaining ingredients and mix well.

If using in sandwich, try adding sliced cucumber either plain or pickled.

HUEVOS RANCHEROS

Corn tortillas—recipe called for the old technique of dipping tortillas into oil in skillet briefly. Instead I sprayed a cookie sheet, then sprayed each tortilla separately. For crisper tortillas do not overlap. This serves six, one tortilla each.

INGREDIENTS:

Six corn tortillas

Ranchero or tomatillo sauce—prepared or make your own (see Condiments section)

2 14 oz. cans pinto beans, drained and rinsed

Grated cheddar

10 Eggs

DIRECTIONS:

Preheat oven to 400°

Lay tortillas on cookie sheet and bake to crisp, working in batches to fit your toaster oven. Mix beans and tomatillo sauce; spread over tortillas. Cover sauce/bean mixture with grated cheese. Bake until cheese is melted and dish is heated through.

Meantime cook eggs, either by poaching or frying, to your taste in doneness. Remove tortilla from oven and top with eggs. Pass extra sauce.

HAM SALAD

I love this recipe because it combines two of my favorite foods: ham and cream cheese. I whir the ham on the chop setting in my counter-top food processor. Just be sure not to over-process until it turns to mush.

INGREDIENTS:

4 oz. cream cheese, softened

2 scallions, chopped

2 Tbsp. chopped parsley

1 Tbsp. mustard—Dijon, Creole, your preference

¼ tsp. cayenne, scant

1/8 tsp. black pepper

8 oz. cooked ham, chopped fine

DIRECTIONS:

Mix it all together. Serve as sandwich filling or with crackers.

ITALIAN OPEN-FACED TUNA SANDWICH

Serves 2

INGREDIENTS:

FOR THE SALSA:

1 cup flat parsley leaves, washed and dried

½ cup olive oil, more if needed

2 garlic cloves,

2 anchovy filets

1 Tbsp. capers, chopped

Zest of 1 lemon

Pinch of crushed red pepper

Salt and pepper to taste

FOR THE SANDWICH:

1 baguette or 2 ciabatta rolls, split

Lettuce or watercress

8 oz. chunk albacore tuna in water, drained,

4 hard cooked eggs, sliced

Salt and pepper

DIRECTIONS:

Make a salsa. Blend parsley and oil in food processor. Add remaining salsa ingredients and season with salt and pepper as needed.

Make the sandwich. Layer ingredients on half of each roll. Pour salsa over.

Serve open face, preferably with a knife and fork.

MUSHROOMS ON TOAST

Mom served mushrooms on toast when I was a kid. Also asparagus on toast, and I always thought the toast thing was British and she was serving it to please my dad. Turns out many cultures serve variations, but I was delighted when such recipes became trendy again. I like the simple method.

Another tiny house cooking caution: your kitchen may be different (I hope it is) but if I use the toaster oven and the hot plate simultaneously I blow a fuse. So do the toast first—it will keep.

INGREDIENTS:

8 oz. bella mushrooms (you can mix in wild mushrooms if the budget will stand it). Clean the mushrooms with a damp paper towel and slice; I only buy pre-sliced in desperation.

Good white bread, toasted

Butter as needed

Salt and pepper to taste

DIRECTIONS:

Couldn't be easier. Melt the butter, cook the mushrooms over medium heat until limp. Add more butter if needed. You want a rich pan sauce that the toast can soak up.

Great opportunities for variation: add a splash of Worestershire; slice a scallion and add; add a bit of white wine; season with thyme and/or rosemary; add about 1/8 cup crème fraiche or heavy cream. Some cooks thicken the sauce with flour, but I suspect that would detract from the mushrooms which are so good themselves.

Serves 2

ASPARAGUS ON TOAST

INGREDIENTS:

Asparagus

Good white bread, toasted

Butter as needed

Salt and pepper to taste

DIRECTIONS:

Steam the asparagus to crisp-tender; drain and rinse with cold water. Cut into manageable pieces. Melt the butter, cook the asparagus over medium heat until limp. Add more butter if needed. You want a rich pan sauce that the toast can soak up.

Mound on toast.

BEANS ON TOAST

Never had these in my childhood home—we didn't eat beans except the sweet baked beans of the North—so when I first saw a recipe for these, I thought I'd discovered something wonderful. A new, trendy recipe. Well it is trendy, but apparently not new. I planned to serve it as something special to a colleague, who was just a bit scornful and said, "Isn't that what we ate as a kid?"

Nonetheless, my son Jamie and I fixed these once when he spent the day with me. He, bless him, cooked the beans overnight at home and brought them to Fort Worth from Dallas.

NATCHITOCHES MEAT PIES

Thanks to Don Oatman of Jefferson TX, who years ago brought these to a pot-luck supper for a writing class I taught. When I couldn't find the recipe for this book, Don scoured around and sent it to me. I have to say Don made dough from scratch, but I always came out with way more filling than dough, so I've gone the refrigerator biscuit route.

INGREDIENTS:

FILLING:

1-1/2 lbs. ground beef

1-1/2 lbs. ground pork

1 cup chopped scallions, tops and bottoms

1 Tbsp. salt

1 tsp. coarse ground black pepper

1 tsp. coarse ground red pepper

½ tsp. cayenne

½ cup flour

DIRECTIONS:

Combine all except the flour in a Dutch oven; cook until meats lose red color. Thoroughly stir in flour. Cool to room temperature. Drain in colander to get rid of grease and juice.

Use canned refrigerator biscuits, separating each biscuit in half. One tube makes sixteen small pies. Roll each half biscuit out in a circle until thin but not fragile. Place a heaping Tbsp. of meat in each half, fold over, and dampen edges to get them to stick. Then crimp as attractively as you can; the tines of a fork work well. Mine are never pretty. Poke with fork to create steam vents.

Put pies on ungreased cookie sheet. Brush tops with butter. Bake at 425° until crust is golden. Pies will rise as they bake, so don't crowd them on the pan. Bake in batches in toaster oven. You can deep fat fry if you prefer.

ORZO WITH SPINACH, ARTICHOKE HEARTS, AND GOAT CHEESE

Thanks to Heather Hogan Holt, my favorite chef-friend, for this recipe. Mine never turns out as good as hers, but it's good enough.

INGREDIENTS:

½ small box orzo

½ tsp. olive oil

Half bag fresh spinach, roughly chopped and wilted

1 can artichoke hearts, roughly chopped (I prefer canned to frozen)

Crème fraiche

Goat cheese

DIRECTIONS:

Cook orzo according to directions, drain, and coat with olive oil to keep it from clumping. Mix in spinach and artichokes and heat, stirring. Remove from burner to pour in enough crème fraiche to bind and crumble in goat cheese.

LEEK/PESTO/RICOTTA PIE

Perfect for brunch, this may be made a day ahead and chilled. Serve at room temperature. Before you start, be sure your pie shell or dish fits in your toaster-oven.

INGREDIENTS:

1 unbaked, prepared pie shell

2 Tbsp. butter

1 large leek

2 large eggs

2 egg whites

¼ cup cream

1 cup ricotta

½ cup grated Parmesan

3 Tbsp. pesto (buy it in the store or make your own)

2 Tbsp. finely chopped fresh Italian parsley (don't used dried—it really makes a difference)

¼ tsp. each salt and pepper

DIRECTIONS:

Slice the leek, using only the white and light green part. Leeks collect more dirt than any other vegetable, so be sure to clean thoroughly in all the hidden layers. Sauté in butter; as slices cook, they will separate into rings. Cook until translucent and lightly caramelized. Set aside to cool.

In medium bowl, whisk egg whites and cream together. Add cooled leeks, Parmesan, pesto parsley, salt and pepper. Combine thoroughly and pour into prepared pie shell.

Bake at 375° until filling is firmly set (use a silver knife to test). Cool and serve at room temperature.

POTATO SALAD, SPINACH, AND EGGS

Serves two.

INGREDIENTS:

3/4 lb. fingerling potatoes, washed and halved

Four slices bacon

1 bunch fresh spinach

Lemon juice and Dijon mustard

Four eggs

DIRECTIONS:

Fry the bacon until crisp. Drain and set aside.

Toss the potatoes with 1 Tbsp. bacon grease and roast at 450 for 30 minutes. Wash, stem, wilt (cook with a tiny bit of water), and drain the spinach, chopping as you drain it. Season with lemon juice and Dijon—perhaps a half lemon and a tsp. Dijon, more to taste. Put sliced potatoes on plates. Top with servings of spinach. Salt the spinach lightly. Poach eggs to individual taste and gently top the potato/spinach mixture. Crumble bacon on top. Serve with salt and pepper for the eggs.

SLOPPY JOE LIKE NO OTHER

When my daughter served this to her husband, he said, "It's good, but it's not sloppy Joe." She wrote me that she supposed she's the only one who grew up thinking red wine was an essential ingredient of sloppy Joe.

INGREDIENTS:

1 lb. ground beef

1 15-oz. can of beans (any kind you want), rinsed and drained

½ cup chopped onion

½ cup diced celery

2 Tbsp. bacon drippings

¼ cups ketchup

1½ Tbsp. Worcestershire sauce

Dash of Tabasco

1 tsp. salt

⅛ tsp. pepper

¼ tsp. oregano

¼ cup dry red wine

1 Tbsp. A-1 sauce

DIRECTIONS:

Cook onion in bacon drippings. Add beef and brown. Add remaining ingredients and simmer 20 to 30 minutes. Serve on toasted buns or in bowls.

SMOKED SALMON AND POTATO SALAD

This is a great, distinctive, and pretty platter to put out for two or three guests or a summer night—if you're sure they like smoked salmon as much as you do.

INGREDIENTS:

1 lb. new potatoes, cooked and peeled (this might be another of those rare cases where canned sliced white potatoes work best).

Salt and pepper

Juice and zest of one lemon

A splash of white wine vinegar

Olive oil

Capers, rinsed and drained

2 tsp. horseradish

¾ cup créme fraiche (substitute sour cream if you must or make your own crème fraiche: see note in Condiments section)

¾ lb. smoked salmon, separated into bite size pieces

DIRECTIONS:

Boil potatoes until just cooked; peel and dress while still warm (if using canned, perhaps heat in microwave just a bit—warm potatoes absorb dressing better).

Mix all of lemon zest and half the juice, vinegar, and olive oil (remember the 3:1 proportion of oil to acid) and whisk to mix. Pour over potatoes.

Separately mix horseradish into crème fraiche. Stir in remaining lemon juice. Salt and pepper to taste.

Lay out salmon pieces on platter. Spoon potatoes (arranging artfully) and any dressing left over them. Drizzle crème fraiche dressing over all and sprinkle with chopped dill.

SPANISH TORTILLA

We often call this traditional Spanish and South American dish a Spanish omelet, but its original name is tortilla Española or *tortilla de patatas.* Often served cold as an appetizer, it first appeared on menus in this country when tapas became popular.

INGREDIENTS:

3 tsp. olive oil, divided

1 small onion, thinly sliced

1 cup cooked potatoes, diced

1 tsp. dried thyme, or 1 Tbsp. fresh

½ tsp. paprika

6 large eggs

4 egg whites

½ cup grated Manchego cheese

2 cups baby spinach, chopped

½ tsp. each salt and finely ground black pepper

DIRECTIONS:

Sauté onion in 2 tsp. olive oil until translucent; add potatoes, paprika and thyme, and sauté briefly.

In good-sized mixing bowl, gently whip whole eggs and whites and then fold into the potato mixture, along with the spinach, cheese, and salt and pepper. Add remaining tsp. olive oil to skillet and put egg/potato mixture in the pan. Cook until potato/egg mixture is set (run a silver knife into the middle to check—bottom should be lightly browned. About five minutes is usually good. Do not let it burn. Serve warm or cold.

May be made a day ahead and stored in the fridge.

TUNA PASTIES

This is a real favorite of mine. Unfortunately, these don't keep well, even in the freezer. But hot from the oven? Delicious!

INGREDIENTS:

1 7 oz. can albacore tuna, in water

1 cup shredded cheddar

¼ cup celery, diced finely

1 Tbsp. fresh parsley, chopped

1/3 cup sour cream

1 pkg. refrigerated biscuit dough

Melted butter

DIRECTIONS:

Mix first five ingredients together. Roll out biscuits until thin. Divide tuna mixture evenly between four biscuits. Top with remaining four biscuits and press to seal edges. Brush with melted butter. If you want appetizer-sized pasties, put a smaller amount of tuna on one side of each biscuit half; fold biscuit over and crimp edges. In either case, poke holes to vent steam as they cook.

Bake at 400° on ungreased cookie sheet for 15 minutes.

VEGETABLE STIR-FRY

This says it serves four to six, but I think you're lucky if you get four servings out of it. You can add more vegetables, but don't add so many that the sauce won't cover them.

INGREDIENTS:

½ cup chicken broth

2-3 Tbsp. soy sauce, low sodium

1 Tbsp. corn starch

2 Tbsp. oil

1 tsp. grated fresh ginger

1 clove garlic, minced

3 cups vegetables—bamboo shoots, bean sprouts, sugar snap peas, thinly sliced onion, sliced summer squash or zucchini, grated carrot, sliced mushrooms, sliced water chestnuts. If you want to use broccoli flowerets, celery, cauliflower, or bell pepper, precook them until tender.

DIRECTIONS:

Mix broth, soy and corn starch and set aside; Heat oil in wok or large skillet; sauté ginger and garlic until fragrant—do not let them burn. Add vegetables and sauté until semi-soft. Pour in broth mixture and cook over medium heat until it thickens and is clear.

Serve as is or over rice; If you are feeding a carnivore, throw in about two cups thinly sliced chicken pieces.

Soups & Salads

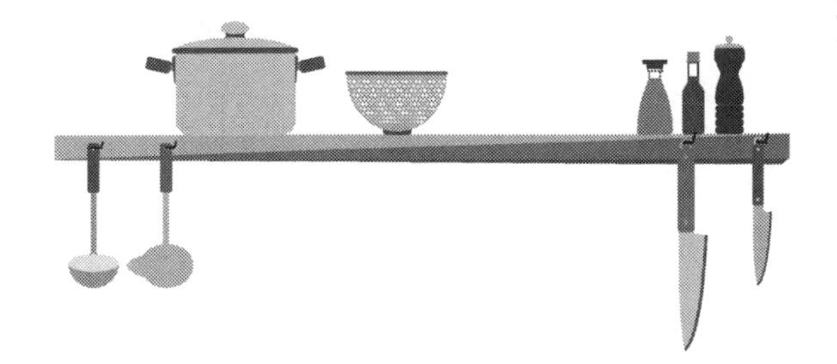

BROCCOLI-CHEESE SOUP

INGREDIENTS:

1-1/2 lbs. broccoli, chopped, fresh or frozen

2 c, half and half

2 cups water

1 lb. Velveeta™, cubed

½ tsp. each salt and pepper

1 cup cold water

½ cup cornstarch

DIRECTIONS:

Cook broccoli, half and half, water, and cheese until cheese is melted, being careful not to scorch. If you have a double boiler, use it; if you have a microwave, use it; if neither, put on low heat and stir constantly—both half and half and cheese will scorch easily. Stir cornstarch into cold water until smooth and then add to soup mixture. Cook over low heat until soup thickens.

HEARTY CHEESEBURGER SOUP

This serves a crowd, if you pack them into your tiny space. You could probably halve it, because it's hearty and filling, but so good.

INGREDIENTS:

2 carrots, grated

1 onion, chopped

2 stalks celery, chopped

3 large baking potatoes, cooked and diced

5 cups chicken broth

¼ cup flour

1/2 cup butter

1 lb. hamburger meat

1/2 cup milk

1 lb. Velveeta™ cheese, cut in chunks

1/4 cup sour cream

Salt and pepper to taste

DIRECTIONS:

Brown the meat, drain and set aside. Dice the potatoes, grate the carrots, and chop the celery and onion. Melt ¼ cup butter in a large pot; sauté the onions and celery until clear. Add carrots, hamburger, potatoes and chicken broth.

Separately, melt remaining ¼ cup butter and stir in flour. Add to soup to thicken. Stir, then add the cheese in chunks and the milk. Stir until cheese is melted. Simmer in crockpot the rest of the day. Just before serving take it off the heat, add sour cream, stir and serve immediately.

LEMONY LENTIL SOUP

I thought I never cooked with lentils, but I found an open half pack in my pantry drawer. So when you find lentils, make soup.

INGREDIENTS:

1 large onion

2 cloves garlic

3 Tbsp. olive oil

1 Tbsp. tomato paste

1 tsp. ground cumin

Pinch of chili powder (optional)

Salt and pepper to taste

4 cups chicken broth

1 cup lentils

2 cups water

1 large carrot, peeled and sliced

Lemon juice to taste, about half a lemon

Fresh chopped cilantro to taste

DIRECTIONS:

Chop the onion fairly fine. Heat the oil in a soup pot and add the diced onion. Using the garlic press, add garlic (have you ever tried to dice garlic? Hard, and who wants to eat those little bits?). Sauté until onion begins to brown.

Add tomato paste, cumin, chili powder, salt and pepper, and cook until spices release their fragrance.

Stir in broth, water, lentils, and carrots. Cook partially covered over medium-low heat. Lentils take longer than you think to soften, so count on letting it simmer for three hours.

At this point, it's easiest to cool the soup and refrigerate it overnight. Next day, put about half in a processor—I work in batches with my countertop blender. Add back into the soup. Heat.

Just before serving, add lemon juice and cilantro.

SUPER-EASY BLACK BEAN SOUP

Warning: I blended this in small batches in my countertop food processor, but the first time I did it, I put too much soup in at one time and it ran all over everywhere. Caution is advised.

INGREDIENTS:

3 Tbsp. olive oil

1 medium onion, diced

1 Tbsp. ground cumin

2-3 cloves garlic, pressed

2 cups beef broth

1 32 oz. can black beans

DIRECTIONS:

Rinse beans and let drain in colander.

Sauté onion in olive oil. When it is translucent, add cumin and cook until spice releases its flavor. Add pressed garlic and cook a minute more.

Add broth to onion/garlic/cumin. Some recipes use chicken broth, but I like the heartiness of beef. Add half the beans, bring to simmer, and take off the heat to cool.

When cool, blend in batches. Return to burner. Add remaining beans and simmer.

Serve hot or cold with sour cream and chopped cilantro or chives for garnish.

SOUP OF THE WEEK

This is something my mom made, and I carried on the tradition. You might think that kids, usually picky about identifying what they eat, would be hesitant about this, but my kids loved it. No matter what, it always seemed to come out brown, but that was okay in Texas where we're known for brown food anyway—beef, beans, chicken-fried steak, and the like.

Save even the tiniest bit of leftovers. Since you're feeding yourself and maybe one other regularly, leftovers won't accumulate quickly enough to keep individually in the freezer so make a soup odds-and-ends container. Got spinach casserole left one night? Put it in that container and freeze. Some chopped steak a few nights later? Dump it on the spinach and freeze.

You have to use a bit of common sense here. Maybe start two soup containers—in Texas, we'd have one for chili, beans, things with that Mexican flavor to them, and another for meat-and-potatoes kinds of dishes.

To make soup: Defrost your odds and ends when you have enough. You'll probably need something to bind them together as soup, so always keep broth (beef, chicken or vegetable) on hand (I prefer the kind in the box—freeze any opened but unused—or the concentrate you keep in the refrigerator) and canned, diced tomatoes. Use one or both.

If you need to add to your soup pot, frozen corn is a great addition, along with frozen petite peas. Dice carrots, onion, celery, or cooked potatoes—whatever you want. Let it simmer all day in a low crockpot. Season to taste—salt, pepper, garlic powder, herbs; cumin and oregano if you're going for a chili or enchilada-based soup.

Leftovers? Use them to start a new soup.

TOMATO SOUP WITH CILANTRO

INGREDIENTS:

1 bunch cilantro

3 Tbsp. olive oil

1 large onion, chopped

2 or 3 garlic cloves

½ cup tomato paste

1-1/2 tsp. cumin

1 tsp. paprika

1 28 oz. can diced tomatoes with liquid

Salt and pepper to taste

Juice of one lime

DIRECTIONS:

Wash and dry cilantro. Reserve a few attractive leaves for garnish and use kitchen twine to tie the rest of the cilantro into a bundle. Set aside.

Heat oil in large, heavy pot. Add onion and sauté until soft and golden. Reduce heat to keep from scorching onion. Add garlic and cook stirring, for a minute, then add tomato paste and spices and cook until paste darkens. Add tomatoes, water, salt and pepper and cilantro bundle. Bring to a boil. Lower heat and simmer 30 minutes, covered. Remove from heat and let cool.

When soup is cool enough to handle, remove cilantro bundle and discard. Using hand-held mixer blend soup until smooth. Chill overnight. Garnish with reserved cilantro at serving. Serve chilled or warm.

TORTILLA SOUP

INGREDIENTS:

6 corn tortillas

2 tsp. olive oil

3 cups chicken broth

1 14 oz. can diced tomatoes, with juice

1 bay leaf

1 garlic clove, pressed

½ tsp. cumin

1/8 tsp. cayenne

1 full chicken breast, skinless, boneless, cut into small strips

1 scallion, thinly sliced

½ cup chopped fresh cilantro

2 Tbsp. fresh lime juice, or to taste

DIRECTIONS:

Brush one side of tortillas with olive oil; stack and cut in half; stack halves and cut into small strips crosswise. Spread strips on baking sheet, Bake at 350° for 15 minutes or until light golden. Set aside.

Heat together broth, bay leaf, garlic, cumin, cayenne; bring to boil and simmer a few minutes. Add chicken and simmer until meat is just cooked through. Add scallion, cilantro, and lime juice. Season with salt and pepper.

When serving, distribute tortilla strips among bowls.

COMPOSED SALADS

No, composed salads are not those jellied concoctions that were popular in your grandma's day and showed up on her table every Sunday when you were a kid. Remember? Orange Jell-O with grated carrots and pineapple chunks? Cherry Jell-O with dark cherries and—shhh!—port wine. Or jellied gazpacho. (I really liked some of those, though pistachio and Cool Whip were a bit much for me.)

Composed salads are simply salads where the ingredients are laid out on a plate instead of tossed in a bowl. Traditionally when you serve them at home, you lay the ingredients out on one large platter. Diners help themselves, but we all know that self-service can get kind of messy. For a small crowd—two to four—I sometimes serve individual salads laid out in a soup plate. You can dress the individual dishes or pass a small pitcher of dressing.

The nice thing about them is you can use almost any ingredients that strike your fancy. There are, however, two basic composed salads familiar to everyone who has ever had lunch in a bistro café. Both of these are often served on a bed of lettuce.

COBB SALAD

Cobb salad started in the 1930s at the Brown Derby restaurant in Hollywood. Owner Bob Cobb went prowling in his restaurant's refrigerator for leftovers, arranged them on a plate, drizzled French dressing over the dish, and there it was. Within days it was on the menu

Traditional ingredients are cold chicken breast, often diced, tomato (cherry tomatoes are good), green beans, tiny potatoes, cheese (sometimes blue, sometimes cheddar), avocado, bacon bits, sometimes artichoke hearts.

Cobb used French dressing on his salad, but use your imagination. I think a good vinaigrette is nice because it accents the flavor of the ingredients without overwhelming them. But restaurants frequently offer a choice, so feel free to use ranch, blue cheese, Italian, honey-mustard, whatever suits.

SALADE NIÇOISE

Whereas Cobb features chicken, salade Niçoise is built around tuna. I like to do it with high quality canned albacore in water. See my note on tuna.

Olives are also traditional, but I omit them because olives are on the short list of things I just don't eat. But tiny baby potatoes, peeled, boiled, and cut in quarters if necessary, green beans, hard-boiled eggs are all common. I sometimes add asparagus.

Here's a vinaigrette that I frequently use (enough for two individual salads):

INGREDIENTS:

Scant quarter cup chives, or substitute tops only of scallions

2 Tbsp. white wine vinegar

1 small shallot, roughly chopped

½ tsp. honey

½ tsp. Dijon mustard

½ cup vegetable oil

DIRECTIONS:

Put it all in the food processor and whirl until greens are absorbed into dressing.

When the potatoes are warm, pour a small bit of vinaigrette on them. Also dress the greens lightly that you use on the plate. Drizzle remaining dressing over the salad.

AVOCADO SALAD DRESSING

This salad dressing is good on Cobb salads or salade Nicoise as well as a plain green salad.

INGREDIENTS:

1 lg. avocado, soft, ready to use; peeled and cut into chunks

2 tsp. lemon juice

½ cup. Greek yogurt

Hot sauce to taste—I sprinkle a few drops

1/4 cup olive oil

2 garlic cloves

3/4 tsp. salt

DIRECTIONS:

Throw it all in the food processor. The avocado is hard to blend—chunks keep reappearing. It's easier if the avocado is very ripe and soft. You have to scrape down the sides and continue to blend until you don't see chunks. But this is really good and healthy.

CREAMY BLUE CHEESE SALAD DRESSING

This salad dressing is good on Cobb salads or salade Nicoise as well as a plain green salad.

INGREDIENTS:

2 Tbsp. each mayonnaise, sour cream, and buttermilk

1 tsp. lemon juice

¼ tsp. pepper

¼ tsp. Kosher salt

1 anchovy fillet, mashed (optional)

Blue cheese— 2–3 Tbsp. to taste

1 finely chopped scallion

DIRECTIONS:

Mix all ingredients, adding cheese and scallion last. If dressing is too thick, sparingly add more buttermilk.

This is classic for wedge salads but also good on torn leaf lettuce and any number of other good things.

CUCUMBER AND AVOCADO SALAD

INGREDIENTS:

1 medium cucumber, seeded and cubed

2 avocados, diced

4 Tbsp. chopped cilantro

1 clove garlic, minced

2 green onions, chopped

Salt and pepper

Juice of ¼ large lemon

Juice of 1 lime

2 Tbsp. crumbled Feta cheese

DIRECTIONS:

Mix it all together and chill well before serving.

CUCUMBER AND TOMATO SALAD

INGREDIENTS:

2 cucumbers, peeled and sliced thin

½ large red onion, sliced thin

3 Roma tomatoes, sliced thin or chunked

1/3 cup plain Greek yogurt

¼ tsp. Dijon mustard

1 Tbsp. white vinegar (I always have it on hand for cleaning solutions)

2 Tbsp. milk

½ tsp. sugar

A bit of chopped parsley

A bit more chopped dill

Pepper and salt to taste

DIRECTIONS:

Mix together the greek yogurt, dijon mustard, white vinegar, milk, sugar, chopped parsley, chopped dill and salt and pepper.

Stir dressing into vegetables and refrigerate at least half a day. I make it the night before. One guest said, "You know, you think cucumber salad—well, okay. But this is really good."

TABBOULEH

I asked a ten-year-old grandson if he liked tabbouleh, and he replied, "I don't know what it is, but I'll eat it." Such a joy to feed a child like that. He ate three helpings. Then his mother tried to make it, and he didn't like it.

In this country, we think of tabbouleh as a grain dish, with bulgur wheat the main ingredient. But in Lebanon, it's a salad, and the wheat is not the major ingredient.

INGREDIENTS:

½ cup fine grain bulgur

1 tsp. ground sumac (if you can find it)

½ tsp. ground allspice

½ cup boiling water

Kosher salt and pepper

3 Tbsp. lemon juice

1 small shallot, minced

½ tsp. sugar

½ cup olive oil

2 good tomatoes (vine-ripened), diced

4 cups chopped Italian parsley, minced

1 cup mint leaves, minced

DIRECTIONS:

Mix bulgur, allspice, sumac, and ½ tsp. salt. Pour ½ cup boiling water over and let it sit 10 minutes.

Mix lemon juice, shallot, sugar, and ½ tsp. salt in a large bowl. Whisk in olive oil. Stir the bulgur with a fork and add to lemon juice mixture. One at a time, add tomatoes, parsley, and mint, stirring well after each addition to be sure dressing is thoroughly distributed. Serve chilled. Serves four generously. Will keep 24 hours refrigerated.

THE BEST BLUE CHEESE SALAD EVER

This salad goes together backward, but it is so good. Be sure to use an unfinished wooden salad bowl, the more seasoned the better.

INGREDIENTS:

Garlic clove, split

Salt, pepper

Dry mustard

Crumbled blue cheese

Cider vinegar

Olive oil

Greens

DIRECTIONS:

There are no precise measurements for this. Rub the salad bowl with the split sides of the garlic clove and then discard clove. Rub seasonings into the bowl. Crumble blue cheese in the bottom of the bowl and add vinegar. Mash blue cheese into vinegar, with a fork, until it sort of dissolves in the vinegar. Add olive oil. Remember the ratio is generally two or three parts oil to one part vinegar, so judge accordingly. The amount of vinegar you put in determines how much dressing you make. (I frequently end up with way too much dressing, so I simply save it in the fridge for another day; I believe salads should be lightly dressed.)

Add torn greens, toss, and serve.

EASY MARINATED SALAD

Another family favorite I've been serving for years.

INGREDIENTS:

1 can quartered artichoke hearts

1 red onion, sliced thin

1 large can cut green beans (not French style), drained

1 small head broccoli, cut into tiny flowerets

A bunch of baby cut carrots, parboiled

1 can corn, drained

1 can black beans, drained and rinsed

Bottled vinaigrette dressing, your favorite

DIRECTIONS:

You can use whatever else you want—the original recipe left out corn and black beans but called for cauliflower (I couldn't see buying a whole cauliflower, and I'm not particularly fond of it), avocado (which gets lost in the mix), and a shredded head of lettuce (which wilts and ruins the leftovers—without it, the salad is good for days).

Use the bottled salad dressing of your choice. The original recipe called for Kraft Italian.

Let the salad sit several hours or overnight in the refrigerator.

OVERNIGHT SALAD

This came from neighbor Amy Brown. It goes against all my principles of handling lettuce, and it is absolutely delicious.

INGREDIENTS:

1 Tbsp. fresh lemon juice

9 Tbsp. olive oil

6 green onions chopped

1 tsp. seasoned salt (I use regular salt)

4-6 cloves garlic, minced—I mashed four because I don't like finding little bits of garlic in my mouth, and I don't mince well

2 avocados, peeled and cut into chunks

I head romaine lettuce

3/4 cup grated Parmesan

DIRECTIONS:

Use a 9x13 glass baking dish (never metal or aluminum), combine lemon juice, oil, onions, salt and garlic. Add avocado chunks and stir until all is coated well. Tear romaine and layer on top of mixture. Cover with Parmesan. DO NOT STIR AT THIS POINT.

Seal tightly with plastic wrap—I use two layers and then a layer of foil—and refrigerate. Stir just before serving.

PASTA SALAD

For lunch or a light supper, pasta salad is a nice change from summer's potato salads. You can put almost anything you want in it, but here are some starter suggestions.

INGREDIENTS:

Pasta, cooked—you can of course use any pasta, but I like the size of egg noodles; salads often incorporate rigatoni or elbow macaroni or similar larger pastas.

Diced, oooked chicken

Diced celery

Sliced green onions

Halved cherry tomatoes

Bell pepper (if you like it)—red adds a nice touch of color

Artichoke hearts, quartered

Bottled or homemade vinaigrette (I use Newman's Own Vinaigrette)

Mayonnaise (optional)

DIRECTIONS:

Toss all together in a large bowl; add dressing to coat but don't let the salad get soupy. Most of my family prefer the salad dressed with only vinaigrette, but I've added a glop of mayo a time or two. My chef friend/taster likes the way the vinaigrette and mayo work together.

Chill before serving.

WILTED LETTUCE

This is an old and simple recipe from my mom.

INGREDIENTS:

1 slice of bacon per person

Fresh leaf lettuce

Vinegar

DIRECTIONS:

Fry 1 slice bacon per person (and try not to burn it—classic wisdom is when you fry bacon, stand there and watch it; do not wander away to your computer). I find it easiest to dice the bacon with scissors before frying.

Drain bacon; reserve bacon grease.

Tear up fresh leaf lettuce into bite size pieces.

Splash vinegar over the greens (1 part vinegar to 3 parts bacon grease).

Pour warm grease and bacon bits over salad and serve immediately.

Condiments, Staples & Cooking Hints

BACON GREASE

Keep a small jar of pure bacon grease in the fridge. Do not mix in any other pan drippings, etc. Keep it pure bacon grease. A few dishes really need it.

BUTTERMILK

No, I'm not kidding. When you find out how easy it is to make your own buttermilk, you'll wonder why you haven't been doing it forever. Don't drink it? I'll bet you want it for cooking and baking sometimes. One caution: you have to plan ahead, because this takes 48 hours.

INGREDIENTS:

½ cup commercial buttermilk (you've got to start somewhere)

2 cups whole milk

1 tsp. Kosher salt

DIRECTIONS:

Mix and let it sit in a glass jar (no aluminum containers, please) in a warm place or 48 hours. So rich and good.

CRÈME FRAICHE

Crème fraiche, pronounced "krem fresh," is a thick heavy cream widely used in France, where the cream is unpasteurized and contains the "friendly" bacteria necessary to thicken it naturally. Since it does not curdle when boiled, it is the ideal thickener for many sauces and soups. Vegetables (particularly potatoes) benefit from a dollop of it. It also can be served on fresh fruit, cakes, cobblers, and puddings.

To make your own: Place 1 cup heavy or whipping cream, room temperature, and 2 Tbsp. cultured buttermilk at room temperature in a lidded jar, like a Mason jar. Tighten the cover and shake for 15 seconds. Set aside at room temperature (about 70° F.) for 24 hours or until very thick. Stir once or twice during that time. Stir thickened crème fraiche well. Cover and refrigerate at least six hours before serving.

Will last up to two weeks in the refrigerator if jar is tightly sealed.

PESTO

Pine nuts are traditional in pesto, but I prefer our Texas pecans.

INGREDIENTS:

3 cups packed fresh basil leaves

4 cloves garlic, peeled

¾ cup grated Parmesan

½ cup olive oil

¼ cup chopped pecans

½ cup chopped parsley

DIRECTIONS:

Combine all the ingredients in the food processor.

Process until smooth. Will keep in the refrigerator three or four days, but this freezes well. A good trick: get an old-fashioned flexible ice cube tray and fill compartments with pesto When frozen solid, pop the cubes out and store in a baggie for use as needed.

RANCHERO SAUCE

INGREDIENTS:

1 tsp. oil

1/4 cup finely chopped onion

½ small jalapeno, chopped and seeded

1 clove garlic, minced

1/4 teaspoon ground cumin

1 14 oz. can diced tomatoes

Salt and pepper to taste

DIRECTIONS:

Heat the oil in a skillet. Sauté the onion, jalapeno, and garlic for a few minutes to soften. Add the cumin and fry 30 more seconds. Add the tomatoes and some salt and pepper.

Cover the skillet and reduce heat to medium-low. Simmer 5 minutes until the tomatoes are soft. You may need to add a couple tablespoons of water to make a sauce if your tomatoes were not very juicy.

Optional: stir in three or four slices bacon, diced and cooked until crisp.

REMOULADE SAUCE

This is terrific with seafood dishes, especially chilled shellfish. But you can use it on meat.

INGREDIENTS:

¾ cup mayonnaise

2 tsp. Dijon mustard

1-1/2 tsp. whole grain mustard

1 tsp. tarragon vinegar (don't have it? Use cider vinegar; shh! Don't tell.)

A few drops of hot sauce, or to taste

2 tsp. drained small capers

1 Tbsp. chopped fresh parsley

1 scallion, thinly sliced, most of green top discarded

Salt and pepper

DIRECTIONS:

Mix together and chill thoroughly before serving.

SPICY BROWN SUGAR

I have spread this on brie before baking and dusted buttered tortillas with it. Cut the tortillas in strips and bake until just crisp. This gives you basic proportions—increase or decrease as needed.

INGREDIENTS:

½ cup brown sugar

½ tsp. cayenne.

DIRECTIONS:

For brie, slice top coating off cheese but leave coating on sides intact. Cover top with sugar mixture. Bake in a moderate oven for ten minutes, but watch it closely so cheese doesn't run, sugar doesn't melt all over everywhere. Delicious with crackers or baguette slices.

TACO SEASONING

Ever read the ingredients list on your favorite brand of taco seasoning? I bet there are some artificial flavors and colors, some preservatives, a lot of stuff you don't necessarily want to put in your body. Making your own is simple and cheaper. And you probably have most of the ingredients on hand.

INGREDIENTS:

1 Tbsp. chili powder

¼ tsp. garlic powder

¼ tsp. onion power

¼ tsp. oregano

½ tsp. paprika

1 tsp. cumin

1 tsp. salt

1 tsp. finely ground black pepper

Crushed red pepper to taste, optional

DIRECTIONS:

Mix all the ingredients together.

Store it in the freezer between uses.

THOUSAND ISLAND DRESSING

I'm not much for Thousand Island dressing, except for an open-faced sandwich I used to order at a specific restaurant—toast, julienned iceberg lettuce, ham, turkey, Swiss, and Thousand Island dressing. And occasionally there's a recipe that calls for that dressing—like Reuben dip. I never used enough to keep it on hand, and I'm never sure I like the bottled variety. So when I need it, I make my own. You can double or triple these basic proportions.

INGREDIENTS:

2 Tbsp. mayonnaise

1 Tbsp. ketchup

½ tsp. pickle relish (I prefer dill, but you can use sweet)

½ tsp. white vinegar

½ tsp. sugar

1/4 tsp. black pepper.

DIRECTIONS:

Mix all the ingredients together.

TONNATO SAUCE

This is fishy and you probably shouldn't keep it more than three days—you know, visitors and fish grow old in three days—but it's good on cold meat. I find plain chicken breast, for instance, too dry, but this sauce makes it come alive.

INGREDIENTS:

1 cup mayonnaise

½ cup olive oil

6 oz. can tuna in oil, with the oil

3 anchovy filets

2 Tbsp. lemon juice

3 Tbsp. capers, drained

DIRECTIONS:

Put it all in the processor and process until well blended. Great over cold meats, such as turkey or chicken, or over fish. You might want to halve it; then you can use the rest of the tuna for a salad.

TZATZIKI SAUCE

You can use this refreshing sauce many ways—with meat, as a dip with vegetables.

INGREDIENTS:

2 cups yogurt

1 small onion, diced

½ cucumber, peeled, seeded and diced

2 cloves garlic (or one large clove), mashed

1 tsp. lemon juice

DIRECTIONS:

Mix together, and chill thoroughly before serving.

WHITE SAUCE

Once when I suggested white sauce to one of my daughters, she said, "You know I don't know how to do that." Just in case you don't either, it's easy.

INGREDIENTS:

1 Tbsp. butter

1 Tbsp. flour

1 cup milk

DIRECTIONS:

Melt a Tbsp. butter in a skillet. Stir in 1 Tbsp. flour. The mixture will become dry and crumbly. Gradually stir in 1 cup milk, in small amounts, stirring and smoothing out lumps as you go. That makes a small amount, but it gives you the basic proportions. Need two cups? Use 2 Tbsp. flour, butter, and milk.

Staples - Stocking the Tiny Kitchen

IN THE FRIDGE

Bouillon, chicken and beef, jars of condensed

Butter

Cheese, artisan, for drop-in guests

Cottage Cheese

Cream cheese

Eggs

Lemons

Salad vegetables

Sausage, prosciutto, or other appetizer meats

Scallions

White wine

IN THE CUPBOARD

Anchovies

Chocolate, dark, designer bar

Crackers, cocktail variety

Olive oil, good quality (Trader Joe's 100% Extra Virgin)

Pasta

Peanut butter

Tomatoes, canned, diced

Tuna, albacore, in water

Vinegar, cider and wine

IN THE FREEZER

Baguette slices

Parmesan, grated, fresh

Pesto

These ingredients give you enough options for that last-minute meal for one, including a peanut butter sandwich, or for a drop-in guest for happy hour. For instance, pasta, pesto, and Parmesan—you've got a main dish. A hunk of Manchego and some prosciutto plus crackers? You're set for when a neighbor drops in at happy hour. When you stock your kitchen, try to think in groupings of food—tuna? You need scallions, lemon, and mayonnaise for quick tuna salad.

QUICK PICKLED VEGETABLES

Whisk together ¼ cup white wine vinegar, ¼ cup cold water, 1 Tbsp. sugar, and 2 tsp. salt. Add 1 cup sliced vegetables (I like red onion and cucumber, but you could use zucchini, lightly cooked carrots, or tiny clusters of broccoli. Let your imagination go!) Store in a tightly closed glass jar in the refrigerator.

SANDWICH SALADS

My method of making egg, tuna, chicken, or ham salad is fairly standard and basic: the meat chopped fine or flaked in the food processor, green onions chopped, seasoning as desired (lemon, mustard, whatever) and mayo to bind. Makes a quick sandwich.

TOMATO-BASED SAUCES

My mom taught me to always add a pinch of sugar to tomato-based sauces. Her advice was it "rounds the sauce off." Never sure what that meant, but it does improve the flavor. Also consider adding two or three anchovy filets. Those folks who won't eat anchovies won't know they're there, and it gives the sauce an earthy, full flavor (Oops! Have I said that before?)

TUNA, A QUICK NOTE

Years ago in a wonderful cookbook, *Jam Today* by Tod Davies, about cooking out of your garden and cupboard, I read a recommendation for tuna ordered from Fishing Vessel Pisces, a small, family cannery in Oregon. One can, and I was hooked. All fish are line caught without the use of nets, so dolphins swim happily along next to the boat. The water-packed albacore tuna (and salmon when it's available) is cooked once, not twice as are most commercial tunas. You get meaty chunks with great flavor. To order, contact: Daryl & Sally Bogardus, PO Box 812; Coos Bay OR 97420. Or call: 541-266-7336 or 541-821-7117. Tell them Judy in Texas told you to call.

Who is Judy Alter

In another life, I'd like to be a chef. As it is, I was born into an osteopathic medical family in Chicago, with a mother who was a marvelous cook and patient enough about teaching me that she let me make a mess in her kitchen. Then she taught me about cleaning up as you go.

After going to work at fourteen in a hospital, I left thoughts of a medical career behind and majored in English in college because I intended to spend my days reading books while some man would take care of me. That didn't quite work out.

I hold a B.A. from the University of Chicago, an M.Ed. from Truman State University, and a Ph.D., with a special interest in literature of the American West, from Texas Christian University. For thirty years, I worked at TCU Press, almost twenty of them as director. My first book was published in the late 1970s and I have written fiction and nonfiction, for adults and young adults. This is my third cookbook, although I have contributed to others.

I've written mostly fiction about women of the American West—books on Libby Custer, Jessie Benton Frémont, Wild West cowgirl Lucille Mulhall, and Etta Place. In the last few years, I've written thirteen contemporary cozy mysteries, all set in Texas—no surprise there. I've been a Texas resident for over fifty years, and it's the home of my heart. Please see my web page, http://www.judyalter.com, for titles or check Amazon.

And while I was doing all that, I was cooking to feed my four children, myself, and countless dinner guests. I've hosted frequent dinner parties and often fed between fifteen and twenty at Sunday night family dinners.

Today I live in a 600-square-foot cottage and cook with a hot plate and a toaster oven. My four children are grown—gulp! They're in their forties—and my seven grandchildren range in age from nineteen to eleven. I share my cottage with Sophie, the bordoodle (deliberate cross of a miniature poodle with a border collie). And I cook. From scratch.

Going from cooking on a large scale to a tiny kitchen required adjustments—in attitude, in appliances, in recipes. In the two years I've been in my tiny kitchen, I've learned much about cooking and myself. I want to share lessons learned and food explored with those who love to cook but find themselves in a tiny kitchen or perhaps a dorm room or who knows where else.

Bon appétit, my friends.

Index of Recipes

Index of Recipes

Index of Recipes

Index of Recipes

Made in the USA
San Bernardino, CA
08 September 2019